Allotment
Gardening

Allotment
Gardening

Bridgette Saunders

THE CROWOOD PRESS

First published in 2009 by
The Crowood Press Ltd
Ramsbury, Marlborough
Wiltshire SN8 2HR

www.crowood.com

British Library Cataloguing-in-Publication Data
A catalogue record for this book is available from the British Library.

ISBN 978 1 84797 022 0

Typeset by Simon Loxley
Printed and bound in Malaysia by Times Offset (M) Sdn Bhd

Contents

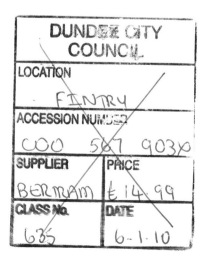

Acknowledgements
There are many people that need a huge thank you for
their help and patience in the evolution of this book:
Ally Penn for helping me to get started; Jan Eaton,
Deborah Kalinke, Deirdre Smith, Sue Chamberlayne and
Julie Hollobone for persistently cheering me on.

A very special thanks to Rhoda Nottridge for her
fantastic photographs taken on many different allotments
and for doggedly trudging through hills and valleys to
capture these images. Most of all I want to thank my
partner Graham Lee for supporting me with this project
and allowing me the space and time to develop this book as
well, making me endless cups of coffee to spur me on and
enabling me to develop my passion for horticulture; also
my lovely children, Josh and Dulcie, for patiently supporting
my emerging computer literacy and for just being there
to encourage me.

The photographer wishes to thank the many allotment-
holders whose plots appear on these pages, especially
those at Hogg's Platt, Roedale, Tenantry Down, Weald
Avenue, West Malvern, Whitehawk Hill and Windmill Hill
allotment sites. I would also like to thank the many other
allotmenteers who offered cups of tea, cabbages, and
gardening wisdom.

This book is dedicated to the author's father,
Derek Saunders, and aunt, Stella Cutting,
whose infinite knowledge of gardening and nature
has been a constant source of inspiration
over many years.

CHAPTER 1

Getting started

HOW AND WHERE TO GET AN ALLOTMENT

Don't be so desperate to get an allotment that you say yes to the first one that you get offered. This is one of the main reasons why people give up their allotment so quickly; in some places up to eighty per cent abandon allotment gardening in the first year! Start off by contacting the allotments officer at your local council, or the National Society of Allotment and Leisure Gardens. Ask for a list of allotments in your area and before making any decisions go and visit them and talk to people with plots there already. The local authority has a statutory obligation to provide allotments where there is a demand.

Don't be put off if there is a long waiting list; by the time some of the people on it get to the top of the list they will have backed out or moved away, so it is worth waiting for the site that you want. Keep in touch with the allotment officer on a regular basis so he or she can be occasionally reminded how keen you are! Having to wait will also give you the opportunity to consider how realistic owning an allotment is to you.

If you know someone who has an allotment, spend some time there 'practising' and see if you like it! If you have a young family, you could also consider sharing your plot with a couple of other families; you are all likely to have little time to spare, and it is much more likely that the children will enjoy it if there are other children there.

A thermos flask or kettle and teapot is an essential piece of kit, so you and your friends can survey your new empire over a cup of tea.

You may have to wait some time for the allotment you really want!

Making a shed out of recycled wood may seem like a good idea at the time, but a bought shed offers more permanence.

CHOOSING YOUR SITE

There are many things to consider when choosing your allotment. Firstly, think about the size of the site – are there lots of allotments there? Does it have a shop? Is it near your house? Will it be realistic to drive three miles every day in the summer to do the watering? People who grow vegetables and flowers in their back garden do not need to plan journeys; they only have to nip outside for five minutes to do some watering, but the allotment-holder will need to organize transport, not just for herself but also for seedlings, compost, tools, and so on. Do try to keep the distance between home and allotment as short as possible.

Think about how much spare time you will realistically have, and think about other commitments that you have at certain times of the year and how this will affect your allotment visits. In the spring and summer you will need at least two hours twice a week, plus four hours at the weekends to work on your allotment. For the rest of the year, things slow down, but if you are going to grow crops all year round you will still need to visit the plot once a week and at the weekend to keep things in check.

Think about the running costs and the money for rent. Allotments are rented on a yearly basis and the standard size of a plot in the UK is 250 square metres. Rents can vary around the country but the most you are likely to pay is still less than £2.00 a week. You will also need to budget for manure and fertilizer, seeds and plants. Hopefully you will recoup the amount spent when you harvest your crop.

Allotment sharing

Sharing the allotment might be the answer to a lack of spare time, and also the inevitability of having far more crops than you or your family can eat, so it is good to be able to share these as well. However, it is

A HISTORY OF ALLOTMENTS

Between 1760 and 1818 over five million acres of land were enclosed, depriving the landless poor of rights over common land. In 1782 an Act was passed enabling guardians of the poor to enclose up to ten acres of waste land for the use of poorhouse inmates.

In 1790, a Private Member's Bill to give small allotments to the poor failed. The General Enclosure Bill of 1796, which provided for land for the poor, also failed. Attempts to introduce allotment legislation failed again in 1800. The 1806 Great Somerford (Wiltshire) Enclosure Act was the first to set aside land as allotment for the labouring poor.

By 1883, seven counties were providing allotments in almost every parish. Then in 1887 an Act came into force that compelled local authorities to provide allotments where a demand was known to exist. However, such obligatory provision only came into force where allotments could not be obtained at a reasonable rent by private treaty.

In 1913, 600,000 allotment plots were recorded in England and Wales, and by 1918 one and a half million allotment plots were available (between 600 square yards and one acre).

During 1919, 7,000 new applicants applied for allotments each week, with a large number of returning ex-servicemen. The Land Settlement Facilities Act, intended to help with provision and reference to 'labouring population', was deleted from the Acts.

In 1922 there was pressure from owners for return of requisitioned land. The Act gave more security and greater compensation to tenants and introduced the concept of an 'allotment garden'. Regulations permitting requisition of land came to an end. The provision of allotments had fallen below one million in 1929, largely due to the loss of requisition land.

In 1930 the National Allotments Society (now the National Society of Allotment and Leisure Gardeners) was formed as the only authoritative national allotment organization.

The war years

During 1939, 570,000 allotment plots were provided in England and Wales, then the 'Dig for Victory' campaign was launched in 1940, when local authorities were eager to help the National Allotments Society.

In 1941, the total annual production on allotments was estimated at 1,300,000 tons and the total produced by newcomers to the allotment movement during the war exceeded three million tons. By the end of 1942, one and a half million allotments were provided and regulations introduced made it an offence to trespass on an allotment.

The Ministry of Agriculture calculated that during 1944, the total annual production on allotments and private gardens contributed ten per cent of all food production in the country.

Post-war allotments

By 1949 The Allotments Advisory Committee recommended that four acres of allotments be provided per 1,000 head of population.

Importantly, in 1950 the Allotments Act extended the length of notice to quit and required local authorities to provide allotment gardens only. The Act also removed contractual restrictions on keeping hens and rabbits on an allotment. This means that hens and rabbits may be kept on an allotment as long as they are not being sold for business purposes. In other words, you must either eat them or keep hens for eggs. If you do keep them, do be aware that the buildings or structures, in accordance with the Allotment Act, must be well maintained (there is also the problem of rats and mice to bear in mind).

During the 1960s much allotment land was sold to developers, but today allotment gardening is becoming increasingly popular again.

really important to agree on boundaries before you do this. You could share a full plot – half and half. This allows for autonomy over the crops you grow, layout, etc. Or you could garden together, in which case it is important to make sure that each person is going to commit the same amount of time to the plot each week. If not this can quickly lead to resentment and that is the last thing you need when gardening is supposed to be therapeutic!

There are many advantages to sharing a plot, such as the sheer enjoyment of working with a friend. It is much less daunting to work with some-one and you can share information, knowledge, enthusiasm and disappointments. Agree on the way you are going to approach the allotment and make sure you are both equally involved in the planning stage. Equality on the allotment is a must. If you don't want to share in this way, consider half a plot to begin with.

Remember if you choose a hillside plot you may need to terrace the ground, but this can be very hard work and a big project to take on board.

Questions to ask, things to look out for

Make sure to read the allotment rules; for example, are there any restrictions on what you can grow?

Ask what the soil conditions are like; you can soon see this by looking around you at what is growing. Check that the site is secure; there is noth-ing worse than your hard work getting constantly damaged and your sheds and greenhouses being vandalized. A padlocked gate is essential wherever your allotment is situated.

Check the plots either side of yours. Don't forget that weeds spread very easily on allotment sites, and things such as brambles, couch grass, bindweed, etc., have a great ability to creep over from one plot to another. If you are an organic gardener, you may want to check if pesticides are being used by your neighbours.

If you have children, you may need to make investigations into any dangerous places on the site, rusty tins, old fridges, etc.

Ensure you are near a water supply. It can be hideous having to carry heavy watering cans up a hill every day to water your crops. Find out if the water is turned off in the winter and think about the implications for that if you are intending to grow winter crops.

Which way does the plot face? For instance, if you intend spending time on your plot on a summer evening, you might want to consider a sheltered plot with a west-facing corner that gets the evening sun. Are there many overhanging trees? A little shade is good, but a totally shady spot is no good for growing flowers and vegetables. Other points to consider include what arrangements are needed for getting rid of rubbish and recycling weeds. Is manure available? Is it a safe place to be alone?

Make sure you know who is responsible for maintaining the hedges and fences about the actual site. The paths between each plot are usually the joint responsibility of you and your neighbour.

Find out about the local allotment society. This often a good place to meet and swap information, and hopefully the allotment shop will sell materials and fertilizers, etc. at a cheaper price than the garden centre.

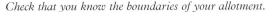

Check that you know the boundaries of your allotment.

CHAPTER 2

Making plans

DRAWING A PLAN

You may find it useful to begin to design your allotment by drawing three plans – the first one showing how the allotment is now, the second showing how you would finally like to plot to be and the third being a short-term plan, showing what you realistically hope to achieve in the first few months. You need to consider how much time and money you have available to start the work.

The initial plan

Take some time to make a fairly accurate scale plan, on graph or squared paper. This will come in handy over the years, and will give you something to aim for. It will help you when you need to calculate things like where to put a new shed or glasshouse and how many plants you need for a certain piece of land.

Try to include as much information about the existing piece of land as you can. Start by drawing the boundaries; it might be a good idea to check with the lease agreement to make sure where the boundaries are. Check what direction the plot is facing; you can do this by using a compass, getting hold of a large-scale map or asking other allotment-holders. Check where the entrance to the allotment is and decide if it is big enough for any deliveries of manure, etc. Check the direction of the prevailing winds. It is usually south-westerly, but this may vary in some locations. This is important when you are thinking about the height of the hedges, and the need for a windbreak, and also when

It is a good idea to have somewhere to sit where you can make plans.

planning the location of fruit bushes. Note any gaps in the hedges.

Make sure you show the paths and how wide they are, and note where the difficult weeds are. Mark areas that have any existing plants on them. Make a note of what they are – for example, if there is rhubarb when you first get your allotment you may not be able to see it in winter so it would be useful to note its location. Draw in water butts, sheds, cold frames and variations in soil, e.g. if a part is very thin chalk or waterlogged.

The second plan

The second plan of how you eventually want your plot to look should include information such as the crops you want to grow, how you will achieve privacy if you want it, and perhaps an area to relax in as well as to garden. You need to make the allotment an attractive place to come to, even in the coldest of weathers. There is nothing wrong with dreaming and even if you manage to achieve only part of your dream, then that's great! So if you fancy a sun-lounger, net curtains and a rose bower, go ahead and draw it on your final plan.

However, do be realistic about how long it might take to achieve your dream, and also how much it might cost.

The third plan

As for your short-term plan, there may not be enough time to clear all the weeds in the first year, but operating a bed system will help you to keep on track and not get overwhelmed with this. Be realistic about what you feel you can achieve in the short term.

Raised beds make the task of maintaining the allotment easier.

RAISED BEDS

I cannot emphasize enough the importance of raised beds when planning your allotment, because they make the task of maintaining the allotment seemingly much easier. Most allotments are large areas to keep under control and raised beds give the gardener the illusion of a less overwhelming space to maintain. One is much more likely to garden a small area at one time. Beds are sometimes provided by allotment societies, for gardeners with disabilities.

Raised beds are particularly useful for gardening all year round; if they are made to the correct measurements, you don't need to walk on them. Therefore, they should be accessible from all sides

and measure 4ft x 6ft (1.2m x 2m). They are also good for crop rotation in that you can contain your crops within the beds.

You are less likely to experience pest damage when using raised beds, as you can easily cover the crops with horticultural fleece, environ mesh or cloches. It is also another barrier against slugs and snails. Some people like to put copper tape around their beds to keep slugs and snails at bay. I've even known someone make a moat around their raised bed to deter them.

Making a raised bed

Construction of raised beds can be simply done by screwing scaffolding boards together. These can be obtained from your local scaffolding company, because if they have a slight defect they have to be thrown away for health and safety reasons. Of course, railway sleepers can also be used or brick and old breeze blocks – in fact, anything that can retain soil. Make sure the wood has been treated and it should last you a good few years.

PATHS

When planning your allotment, one of the most important things to consider is where to place paths. Making paths will be one of your first allotment tasks; this is an excellent job to do in the winter. There are many different surfaces you can use and it is a great way of recycling things.

Freecycle is a national community exchange of unwanted goods and could be a good source of path materials, but many councils have their own exchange set-ups and people are often getting rid of old slabs, hardcore, etc. – ask around. Of course, slabs can also be used to make bases for sheds or greenhouses.

You can also contact local landscapers if you are looking for slabs or bricks, as they often find it difficult to dispose of unwanted hard landscaping materials. They are often happy for you to take them away for free.

Old wine bottles, shells or roof tiles can also be used to line the sides of pathways. These look lovely in the sunshine and can be used at night for night-light holders as a means of lighting the pathway for a special occasion.

A pathway can be made from all sorts of different materials: old drain covers, gravel, slate, old bricks, pebbles, old tiles, sawn-up logs, etc. These can be arranged in various ways to be both functional and attractive. The pathways need to be temporary, so that they are easily moved around, so avoid using concrete or cement.

Hard landscaped pathways are, of course, there for a reason and it is important to ensure they are wide enough for access with a wheelbarrow. They are much easier to maintain than, say, a grass surface.

Old wine bottles make a good edging for paths.

It is useful to put down weed suppressant membrane before laying paths.

Laying a path

- Dig a trench 4-6in (10-15cm) deep where the path is to be laid.
- Mark out the path using pegs and string.
- Once the path has been pegged out, old carpet or a membrane made for suppressing weeds can be laid. This stops the weeds from coming through.
- Broken-up pallets can be used as a framework for the paths to contain the materials.
- Depending on your circumstances, pathways can be set on a bed of sand or hardcore, if available. Ram the hardcore into place and then add the sand using a board to spread and level it.
- If funds are short, you can lay slabs directly onto carpet and fill in the gaps with soil or sand. The only problem with this method is that if they get very wet they are liable to move. One way of combatting this problem is to plant thyme, *Erigeron* 'Profusion' or mind-your-own-business or another low-growing plant that will knit together in the cracks and prevent weeds.
- Paths can look very effective when several materials are used and this is ideal for the allotment gardener. Don't forget a pathway can be added to as and when materials become available.

WATER CONTAINERS

In the present climate, it goes without saying that harvesting water is essential. When planning the allotment, it is important to site your water butts or containers so they are near to your crops. This avoids a lot of carrying. Many allotments have taps available, which are often turned off during winter, so it is a good idea to provide your own water. Where possible, try to fix guttering to any buildings on the site.

Use any receptacle you can find to catch rainwater, e.g. recycled oil drums or other plastic containers, making sure to clean them before use. You should also have plenty of watering cans available to save your back.

If your allotment is on a slope, site some water butts at the top, then attach a hosepipe to allow you to move around in different areas.

An old oil drum makes an excellent water butt.

COMPOST HEAPS

Considering that around fifty-five per cent of household waste is organic matter, the compost heap is a must for any gardener. The end product will benefit the soil and will save you a lot of time and money. An ideal bin will have solid sides to retain the heat and moisture and a cover to keep out rain and be placed directly onto the soil.

You can build compost bins from old pallets. Remember to treat with preservative so it will last a few years. Other materials that can be used are:

- Old tyres turned inside out and stacked on top of each other.
- A piece of old carpet wrapped round a circle of wire mesh.

An old recycled bedstead helps to contain the compost.

MATERIALS FOR COMPOSTING

- Farmyard manure
- Pet manure and beddings (use only manure from vegetarian pets)
- Vegetable peelings and kitchen scraps (non-cooked)
- Fruit skins
- Coffee grounds and tea bags
- Torn paper and cardboard
- Wood ash
- Natural fibre fabrics, e.g. cotton
- Grass clippings
- Soft plant material e.g. annuals, vegetables and herbaceous plants
- Nettle tops (not the root)

What you cannot compost
- Cooked foods (this will attract rats)
- Persistent and pernicious weeds, such as couch grass (*Agropyron repens*), ground elder (*Aegopodium podagria*) and bindweed (*Convolvulus arvensis*)
- Foam and plastic packaging
- Coal ash

- Breeze blocks, which can make a very sturdy bin.
- Double wire netting, forced around posts, and filled with hay, straw, cardboard or newspaper.

It is important to have more than one bin. You need one for rotting organic matter, one for already rotted matter and another for shreddings from prunings, i.e. woody plants and trees, as these take longer to rot down. If you have a lot of leaves, you can make a separate leaf container. Leaves take longer to rot down and should be kept separately.

SHEDS

Maybe a shed on an allotment is more for shelter and drinking cups of tea, rather than for keeping tools, as they are not always secure for storage.

There is nothing worse than being on an exposed site in the middle of winter with the rain pouring down and the wind blowing with nowhere to shelter. So a shed is a very important part of an allotment.

One allotment-holder famously showed his means of security to about 20m viewers on TV. He had hung a picture in his shed and behind it he had stored his tools. You can buy implements that fit one handle and this may help with security.

There are various ways of acquiring a shed:

- You can build your own using pallets (make sure they are non-returnable).
- Often sheds are advertised in your local paper going very cheaply.
- Even new, you can buy them fairly cheaply from DIY stores.

Inside a shed you can include a number of things to organize your tools, e.g. a tool rack, an old chest with labelled drawers, shelves for pots. Jam jars are also useful where you fix the lid underneath a shelf and then screw the jar up into it. Workbenches can also be made out of pallets – you should make sure they are the correct height for working to avoid putting a strain on your back. A shed is also a good place to keep your labels and string. I keep my string in a tin with a hole in the lid to stop the string getting knotty and to make it easily accessible.

A luxury item in the shed would be a wood burner to keep you warm in the winter. You can sometimes pick these up cheaply. Having a comfortable shed will make going to the allotment in the colder months a much more pleasant experience.

TOOLS AND EQUIPMENT

Don't make the mistake of going out and buying lots of tools before you know exactly what they will be used for. Tools are not cheap – but if they are good quality they should last a long time. It is possible to buy just one handle to which you can fit several implements, e.g. hoe, rake, etc. This is useful if security is an issue, as you can take the handle away – the tools are not so useful without the handle!

The following are the most essential items of equipment for allotment gardening.

Often sheds are advertised in your local paper going very cheaply.

Old tools can always be re-used around the allotment.

Spade

A spade is used for digging, planting and skimming off weeds. Choose your spade very carefully as this is the one item of equipment that has to take the most strain. Make sure you try it out for size before you buy it, and make sure that it is comfortable for you to hold. You are less likely to get blisters if you choose a 'YD' handle, rather than a 'T' shape.

If you have clay soil, you may find that a stainless steel blade is better. The blade of a standard spade is 29cm x 19cm (11in x 7in) and a light one 25cm x 16 cm (10in x 6in). You can get smaller models – they may be more suitable for if you are of small build.

Fork

The fork has the same features as the spade in the form of handgrips and weight or balance. It is useful for digging on heavy or stony soil, handling manure and compost, lifting vegetable crops and breaking down rough-dug soil. The fork can be used in the same way as a spade on heavy or stony earth and it can be helpful on these difficult soils.

I like to use a border fork, sometimes called a 'ladies' fork, as it is lighter and much easier to get into small spaces such as a herbaceous border or in between vegetables. It is also good for 'fluffing up' the soil when you have finished planting.

The potato fork has prongs that may be square or flattened; this was traditionally used for lifting the potato crop.

Rake

A rake is used for levelling and breaking down the soil. You can use it to bash out lumps of soil and also turn it over to smooth over the soil. You can also use the handle to make a seed drill. It is useful for collecting up stones and leaves. It is also a good tool for leaving a good finish to your plot.

The handle of a rake is about 1.5m (5ft) long and is generally made of wood or tubular alloy. It has a 30cm (12in) long head fitted with 5cm (2in) teeth. When buying a rake, make sure the teeth fit solidly to the head and that the handle is smooth.

Hoe

Hoes are such useful tools in the garden and there are various types to choose from that do different jobs. The Dutch hoe has a flat blade attached to a 'horseshoe' of steel at the end of a 1.5m (5ft) handle, and is brilliant for skimming off annual weeds and for drawing drills against a garden line.

A draw hoe is used for earthing up plants as well as weeding.

Remember not to hoe too deeply; just sever the annual weeds from their roots at ground level, not below. Then all you need to do is leave the weeds on the surface to dry out and die in the sun.

Trowel and hand fork

These are useful for container gardening and also planting out vegetables and bedding plants. It really is worth investing in a good trowel rather than the cheap plastic varieties as they need to be comfortable and strong with a securely attached handle made of wood.

Garden line

A garden line is essential for edging lawns, borders and plots and also for setting out drills and generally marking out. It should be made from nylon or cord and should be wound round a steel reel rather than a wooden peg as these eventually rot and snap.

Measuring stick

I use a piece of wood that has been treated with preservative as a measuring stick. Your measuring stick should be 2m or 6ft in length, marked along the edge in units of 30cm (1ft). It needs to be wide enough to use as a kneeler and still be able to see the markings. It is best to make the marks with a saw rather than paint, which often wears away or gets caked in mud.

The fact that this can be used as a kneeler as well makes it a dual-purpose item for the shed.

Secateurs

There are three types of secateurs. One type has a straight-edged blade that cuts down on to a bar of softer metal. The second has an outwardly curving blade that cuts against, but not directly on to, a fixed shaft. The third has two convexly curved blades that cut in a scissor-like manner. They all do the job if they are kept sharp; there is nothing more frustrating than a pair of blunt secateurs that leave a jagged edge.

The other problem I find is they are always getting lost, so it helps to put some brightly-coloured insulating tape around the handle and if you do leave them lying on the grass by mistake this will help you to find them!

CHAPTER 3

Designing and landscaping

How you design your allotment plot is crucial if you are to be successful, and there are many things to consider when both choosing and planning the site. Firstly, you need to consider what exactly you want to achieve.

- Is your allotment just for growing food?
- Do you want to grow flowers and fruit?
- Is it going to be a place to escape to?
- Will you bring friends or children there?
- Is there any privacy?

It is also essential to consider where you will site your beds, etc. If your allotment is on a slope, how will you deal with this? To terrace it may be a very difficult and time-consuming task, but is well worth considering if you intend to stay on your allotment for a long time.

Remember that different plants have different requirements; for example, annuals need plenty of sun and quite a lot of attention, whereas herbaceous perennials and soft fruit are not so particular, while salads will cope with some shade.

HARD LANDSCAPING

Skip foraging is the best way to start when thinking about hard landscaping your allotment! Be sure to ask permission of the skip owner before taking things and be sure to wear gloves to protect yourself from broken glass and nails. Try to find wood for making raised beds, old drawers and old boxes for germinating seeds, glass for cold frame lids and slabs to make paths and possibly a seating area.

The fencing on this allotment was all made by recycling wood from old builder's pallets.

A level plot is always a bonus.

Often skips will contain discarded bricks, which are useful for making paths.

Many areas have wood recycling projects where you can find wood to make compost bins, etc. Pallets are also a good resource for the allotment gardener, but make sure they are the non-returnable ones.

When starting your allotment, it's best to set out

Before choosing your allotment, check where the water tap is.

the hard landscaping areas first before embarking on the soft landscaping, i.e. the plants. If your allotment is on a very sloping site, it may be as well to terrace it. This can be a big job and will require a lot of digging, so consider this when choosing your site.

CROP ROTATION

When you are designing your allotment, it is a good time to think about crop rotation. There are some things that will either make or break your success as a gardener and crop rotation is one of them; get it right and you are away.

There are several benefits to crop rotation, not least because if crops are planted in the same place year after year there will be a build-up of pests and diseases, such as clubroot and of course the dreaded blight. Both of these diseases stay in the soil for up to twenty-five years and more, so it is not something you want to encourage. There are other problems such as onion stem eelworms, and if you continue to plant onions in the same place this will cause a build-up of the pest.

Another good reason for crop rotation is that one group of vegetables can benefit the next group; for example, brassicas need nitrogen, and legumes have the ability to fix nitrogen in the soil, therefore it seems sensible to follow your beans and peas with brassicas so they can benefit from the available nitrogen in the soil. A similar thing applies with potatoes and onions; potatoes are good weed suppressers as they have a large canopy of leaves to shade out the weed seedlings, while onions, on the other hand, grow straight up and are not so good at suppressing weeds. For this reason, it is a good idea to follow on your potato crop with onions.

Grouping your crops

The easiest way to practise crop rotation is to sort your vegetables into groups. Plan this out on paper beforehand, as sometimes just thinking about it isn't enough! Grouping your vegetables is another good reason for making beds; crop rotation is much easier if you have one bed for each vegetable group. Try to mark out at least five beds at the planning stage.

You will need a bed for root vegetables. Potatoes are often included with root vegetables, even though potatoes benefit more from organic matter. However, if root vegetables are given too much organic matter and the soil is too rich, this will cause the roots to fork and produce more green growth than roots. For this reason I think it is best to keep them separate. Another large bed should be kept for permanent vegetables; this should include globe artichokes (Jerusalem artichokes are best grown around the edge of the allotment as a wind break), asparagus, rhubarb and sea kale. Other crops such as sweet corn and spinach can be fitted in where there is space, but before sowing think about the individual needs of the plant.

To summarize, you will need one bed for brassicas, one for legumes, one for roots, one for onions, one for potatoes and one for permanent vegetables. The permanent vegetables are perennials and therefore will not be moved to other beds, but the others should be rotated; in this way no group is grown in the same soil for more than one season.

Preparation

Don't forget that different types of vegetable require different kinds of preparation of the beds they are to grow in. For example, potatoes need a deeply cultivated soil, as it will be moved a lot when the potatoes are being earthed up; on the other hand, carrots, parsnips and beetroot need a much

Crops grown in rows is the more traditional way of using allotment space.

firmer and level soil as this will not need to be moved during the growing season. Other crops need the soil manuring or liming.

Catch cropping and intercropping

Another method of utilizing the space available is the practice of catch cropping and intercropping. Some vegetables are slower to mature than others, resulting in gaps in land use where the quicker-maturing plants have already cropped. These can be used to 'catch' a crop in the rotation plan; for

example, when peas have finished growing, the ground may not be needed for brassicas until the following spring, so other vegetables such as radishes or endive could be planted.

Intercropping is where you have a slow-maturing vegetable that occupies the ground for many weeks, for example leeks and parsnips. Sow spinach, radishes, spring onions or lettuces in between these crops. It also helps to identify where you have sown slow-germinating seeds such as parsnips if quick-growing spring onions are sown by their side.

Left: An unusual design for a herb bed.

Below: Angelica makes a fantastic architectural plant, as well as a useful herb.

HERBS

If you look in the *RHS Encyclopedia of Herbs* you will come across over 1,000 species, varieties and cultivars of herb. Loosely speaking, when we are referring to herbs we usually mean something that is used for either culinary, medicinal or aromatic use.

Herbs are wonderful to grow on your allotment: many will tolerate some neglect of watering if they come from Mediterranean climates, and they are great for attracting bees and butterflies, which in turn will assist pollination of your other plants. There are also herbs that will tolerate shade and some moisture, such as angelica, chervil, mint, parsley and sorrel, so you may want to site these in another suitable area of your allotment.

Try to keep your perennial herbs, such as rosemary, sage, thyme, chives and marjoram, in a separate bed from the annuals, such as borage, dill, basil, etc. Make sure you familiarize yourself with the life cycle of the herbs, as they will require different conditions and care.

Make sure you find out the size and eventual spread of your herbs and also make sure you can get to them for picking and cutting, as many of

Lavender is easy to propagate from cuttings…

…and can also be used to create a low aromatic hedge.

them make great cut flowers as well. Some herbs, such as mint and lemon balm, are very invasive and so make sure you contain their roots in a bucket or flower pot planted underground.

It is well to remember that some herbs are annuals and will not tolerate cold, wind or frost. Tender plants such as basil need to be sown under glass with some heat to enable germination. They can be planted out into a very sheltered spot in the allotment or grown in the greenhouse along the edge of the tomatoes. Keep pinching out the tops once they have grown and this will encourage new growth to keep you going throughout the summer.

Other herbs such as rosemary and cotton lavender can be used to make boundary hedges.

I like to use old olive oil tins for my annual herbs, as they give a great Mediterranean look and there are some wonderful designs on tins from delicatessens and Turkish and Greek supermarkets. Do be sure to make drainage holes in the bottom.

PROPAGATING HERBS

It is easy to propagate herbs such as rosemary and lavender by taking cuttings at almost any time of the year. To do this, take a cutting underneath a leaf joint (node) using a sharp knife. The cutting can be just a few centimetres long in the case of thyme or up to 10cm in the case of rosemary. Much will depend on what time of year you take your cuttings. If you look carefully at the plant you can see how much soft wood there is, by looking at the change of colour from soft wood to ripened wood; it is the soft wood that you need.

Insert your cutting into a mixture of compost and horticultural grit, to enable the plants to put down roots and to allow the water to drain freely, thus preventing rotting. You can either use recycled yoghurt pots or small flower pots to put your cuttings in. I sometimes use the plastic punnets that strawberries come in from the supermarket; they even have drainage holes in the bottom. (The more shallow ones are good for sowing seeds into.) It is also possible to take cuttings with a heel, pulling down a side shoot so you get a piece of ripened wood as well; trim this 'tail' up with a sharp knife and then insert into the compost.

Make sure you only use commercially bought compost for propagation. Compost from your compost heap will be too rich for cuttings and seeds and also possibly contain weed seeds. These plants will root in a cold frame or glasshouse, but soft cuttings will need to be misted using a hand-held spray or they will lose a lot of water and start to flop. The semi-ripe wood with a heel will not lose water so quickly so it is more likely to survive. Try to keep your cuttings watered and check on them regularly, keeping a note in the diary of how they are doing. When they have rooted, which may take several weeks if you have no bottom heat, pot them into a bigger pot – the next size up will do fine. However, if you are lucky enough to have access to a heated bench frame these cuttings will only take a few weeks to put down roots.

When they have developed really good roots plant them out, making sure you prepare the planting hole well first and make certain the area has been well weeded, fed and watered.

Rosemary is excellent for attracting bees.

If you prefer, you can just plant herbs amongst your vegetables, potager-style. A potager garden is a French method of creating an ornamental vegetable or kitchen garden. Often flowers (edible and non-edible) and herbs are planted with vegetables. This is great for encouraging pollinating insects. Borage, for example, is not only pretty, but if you have it on your allotment you will see that the bees absolutely love it.

Make sure you prune the herbs that are known as sub-shrubs, for example, lavender, rosemary, thyme, cotton lavender, curry plant and sage. If you leave these plants to their own devices they will become very leggy and unattractive. When they have finished flowering, take a pair of shears and just cut off the dead flower heads. In the spring around March-April time take your secateurs and prune the plant back quite hard, but not into the old wood. Run your hands down the plant and look to see where the shoots begin to come out of the stem, count two lots of leaves then cut just above the second lot of leaves. This will make a lovely mound-shaped shrub for the following summer. (The reason for leaving two sets of leaves is that if there is frost damage you can remove the damaged leaves and the next ones will have a chance to recover.) The new shoots that emerge can be used for cuttings, as can the ones you prune off.

Harvest the herbs and use as required; they have so many uses and are a must for the allotment.

TREES

There are often trees surrounding allotment sites. Try to get to know these trees. Are they fruit-producing, for example elder, malus, rowans and sloes? Are they deciduous (losing their leaves in the winter) or evergreen? What kind of shade do they give? Do they support a particular kind of wildlife? They generally need very little attention and grow quite happily for many years. If you enjoy propagating, you could try to grow some on your allotment from seed or cuttings; *Asculum* (horse chestnut), *Fagus* (beech), *Quercus* (oak) and *Sorbus* (mountain ash) will all grow from seed, and *Acer* (maple), *Betula* (birch), *Prunus* (cherry) and *Salix* (willow) will all grow from cuttings. The small trees make good presents!

There are several small trees that are suitable for growing in locations that are restricted, but make sure you check with your allotment provider before making any decisions about growing trees. You can, of course, grow trees in containers but you must keep them well watered if they are to succeed. Some trees grow to only a couple of metres high. *Acer*, *Prunus*, *Malus* and *Gleditsia* all have some small trees in their species, many of which are lovely, but think carefully before purchasing one as they are expensive.

SHRUBS

A shrub is a plant that has a multi-stemmed structure, unlike a tree, which has one main stem, the trunk. Shrubs are excellent plants for the allotment, providing shelter, privacy and year-round interest, whether they be evergreen or deciduous. Some

Sorbus is quick growing and provides food for the birds, and berries to make conserves.

Both Cornus *(dogwood)
and* Salix *(willow) give
winter interest and are easy
to propagate.*

deciduous shrubs such as *cornus* (dogwood) and *salix* (willow) have wonderful coloured stems. There are many different shapes and this needs to be considered when choosing your shrubs. Some such as buddleia attract wildlife, and many, for example berberis (barberry) and cotoneaster, have fantastic berries as well as flowers. There are others, such as *viburnum* and *philadelphus* that smell beautiful. Some such as *Vinca* (periwinkle) and some junipers are good at covering the ground. Some larger shrubs such as *Parrotias persica*

(Persian ironwood) are like small trees and will give shade.

These can be ordered very cheaply by mail order or raised from cuttings. Harwood cuttings are so easy; pencil-thick stems of one-year-old wood should be taken beneath a leaf joint, about 25cm long. This should be done in the autumn when the plant has lost its leaves, usually some time between October and February. Insert the cutting into a piece of spare ground that has been covered in polythene or membrane, and this will give you

Hebes are evergreen and also attract butterflies.

plenty of free shrubs that can be planted out the following autumn.

Salix, Cornus, Philadelphus, Rubus cockburnianus, Buddleia, *Kerria, Deutzia* and *Kolkwitizia* will all work in this way. If you are unfamiliar with these names look them up on the internet or in a good shrub identification book.

Make sure you keep them well watered until they are established. Make sure you check their height and spread before you plant them, and also the soil conditions they require to flourish.

Many of the evergreen shrubs such as *Osmanthus, Hebe, Skimmia* and *Mahonia* also make fine specimens to put near your allotment shed to give some height and interest.

BOUNDARIES

One way of making a boundary fence is to put in stakes of hazel and 'weave' old twigs and pieces of prunings into it until you have made a fence. This is a good way of recycling left-over pieces of wood. Visit your local wood recycling project where you

Wooden woven fencing makes an excellent boundary.

Brachyglottis greyi *is a good choice as a windbreak, especially on a coastal site.*

may well find all sorts of exciting pieces to make your boundary.

Pallets also come in handy as boundaries and there are many creative ways of using them. Tyres stacked alternately can make a boundary and these can be planted with strawberries, potatoes or bedding plants. Fences can be made from vertical poles or stakes conveying a 'keep out' message, wired or braced together as required. The spacing would depend on what you are trying to keep out. For example, if you have a rabbit problem, space them closely together; if not you can be as creative as you like! Versatile bamboo offers another alternative. Bamboo can be tied in a lattice fashion, used vertically or in a woven form. This is something that needs to be done over time, but make sure your post fixings are stable, and use either a metal post 'shoe' or cement your post into the ground.

Hedging

Hedges filter the wind and reduce its strength. A windbreak can provide some protection over an area ten times its height. Hedging is another form of boundary and any shrubs can be used to make a hedge. Things like *Buxus* (box) and *Taxus* (yew) make wonderful hedges, but are usually quite slow-growing and more for the formal garden – but it could be fun to do a bit of topiary using box – a chicken or a train perhaps! Why not use a variety of plants to make a mixed hedge; *Lonicera* (honeysuckle) and *Rosa canina* (dog rose) all make great hedging plants and attract wildlife, and *Prunus spinosa* (blackthorn) has the added extra of producing fruit. These hedging plants are very cheap to buy from mail order catalogues in the back of gardening magazines. You can also use flowering plants such as escallonia, lavender, forsythia and *Rosa rugosa*.

It is best to dig a trench when planting hedges, and use string or canes to make sure you get a straight line. Most hedge plants need about 2 ft (60cm) between plants. Make sure you cut them back by a third on planting; the reason for this is that if you don't you will end up with a straggly hedge with a bare bottom. You want your plants to start producing bushy growth and pruning them will enable them to do this.

On planting the hedge, make sure you incorporate plenty of well-rotted manure; these plants will take up a lot of moisture as they are planted closely together. Once established, hedges often get neglected. Try to water your hedge regularly in the first year and keep it clear of weeds that will compete for food and water.

CHAPTER 4

Soils – getting your hands dirty

TYPES OF SOIL

Soils are classified as acid, neutral or alkaline. This will vary according to the underlying rock where you live, as will the appropriate cultivation techniques for the different soils. The pH scale measures the acidity or alkalinity on a scale of 1 to 14. 7 is a neutral soil; anything below this is acid and above is alkaline.

It is very important to be continually improving the soil structure on your allotment. The soil structure is the way in which the minerals, organic matter and humus (the end product of the rotting-down process) combine together and make larger particles known as aggregates.

Clay

Clay soil is mainly composed of various fine particles that stick closely together and when wet and compressed can become an unworkable mass. Clay soil hangs onto moisture, which makes it difficult to cultivate. In the summer when it is dry, clay becomes very hard and cracks appear on the surface. Clay soils are also slow to warm up in the spring. Although clay can have a satisfactory structure, it can be difficult to maintain. This is because the water can be slow to drain away and this deprives the roots of the plants of oxygen.

If you have an acid clay soil, then you need to add lime annually to help improve the texture. However, it is not a good idea to add manure and lime at the same time. This will deprive the manure of nitrogen, which in turn will slow down the rate at which it decomposes into valuable humus. The best

Bark chippings make an excellent mulch.

DEFINITIONS

These are some terms that are often used when describing the qualities of different types of soil, and you may well come across them in gardening books.

Tilth: a term used to refer to the physical state of the soil. A fine tilth is required for seed-sowing so that the seed can come into contact with the soil particles.
Friable: this word is used to describe a soil that will easily break down into crumbs, which are small round aggregates.
Soil texture: this refers to the consistency of the soil in relation to particle size.
Soil structure: this is the way in which the individual components in the soil are combined to form larger aggregates.
Fertility: this refers to the soil with respect to the amount of nutrients and their availability. Fertility is usually better in a soil with good structure.
Aggregates: combined masses of particles in soil.

way to find out whether or not your clay soil is acidic is to do a soil test. Kits are available from garden centres and DIY shops. The type of clay soil you have is very much dependent upon the underlying rock type, e.g. the South Downs have underlying chalk and consequently the clay soil there is very alkaline. However, be aware of the fact that pockets of different soils may also be found in the one area.

Dry, chalky soil is pale in appearance.

Sand

If you have sandy soil in your allotment, you will find it is very light and very easy to work and in fact you can sometimes pull plants straight out of sandy soil without even having to dig them up. However, it tends to dry out quickly in the summer and also loses nutrients very quickly.

Loam

If you're really lucky, you may have loamy soil, which is ideal for allotment gardening. Unfortunately, not many of us are that lucky. Loam is a combination of clay, sand and maybe some silt, which drains well, but also holds onto sufficient moisture to allow plants to grow well.

Chalk

Chalk in soils means that they are generally very well drained. However, there is usually only a very thin layer of topsoil present, which can make it very difficult to grow certain permanent plants.

WHAT SOIL DO I HAVE?

How do you discover what kind of soil you have? Look at it, feel it, dig it and also make notes of which plants grow well in it. Try out the following checks.

- Look – dark soils are usually rich in organic matter. Pale grey soils suggest chalk with little organic matter. Yellow and red soils are normally sandstone soils that drain well, need feeding and may be acidic. Yellow or orange sticky soils are usually clay. There may be plenty of nutrients in them, but they may be lacking in air. Brown soils are generally clayey loam; in other words, they are good soils if they are kept open and well drained. Soils that are dark and flaky are

Viburnums are examples of calcicoles.

often peaty and that usually means that they are acidic.

- Feel – pick up the soil and rub it between your finger and thumb. If it feels smooth but lumpy, it's clay. If it feels gritty, then it is a coarse or medium sand. If it sticks to your boots, then it is clay; and if it doesn't, then it is sandy. Try crushing it in your hand; if it falls apart when you open your hand it is too sandy. However, if the soil clings loosely together you are lucky – you have loam, the perfect garden soil.
- Dig – if the soil sticks to your spade and turns over in shiny lumps, it is clay. However, if after rainfall you can turn it over and it still falls apart, it is sandy.

As mentioned above, you can also use a soil testing kit, which can be bought quite cheaply from the garden centre. Just follow the instructions on the packet. This is always a good idea if your allotment is on a previously uncultivated area. Try to make several tests in a WW shape across the patch. Most vegetables like a pH of around 6/7, so you will be able to tell after testing whether you need to add lime to raise the pH if it is too acid.

NUTRIENT CONTENT

The impact of pH on the nutrient availability is something the allotment gardener needs to take into consideration. For instance, some nutrients are limited in acid soils and others in alkaline, and this will determine what you are able to grow. Calcium, phosphorus and molybdenum are not readily available on acid soils, while iron, manganese and boron are restricted on alkaline soils. Generally plants will grow best in soils of a pH of 6–7, although most plants will tolerate a higher or lower pH. There are, of course, exceptions. Plants that prefer an acid soil are called calcifuges and include rhododendrons, camellias, ericas and magnolias. These do not survive on an alkaline soil as the nutrients they require to flourish are not available to them in these conditions. Calcicoles, plants that prefer an alkaline soil, include clematis, dianthus, scabious and viburnum, and do well on chalky soil where the nutrients they require are available.

Some green manures are nitrogen-fixing.

It is very difficult to change the pH of a soil, although there are ways in which you can make the soil more alkaline or acid (by using sulphur to reduce the pH and lime to raise it); it is much better to work with what you have got and try to improve the nutrient content and soil structure.

There are three essential nutrients for plant growth.

Nitrogen

N is the chemical symbol for nitrogen. Nitrogen promotes green leafy growth and is important in lawns and leafy crops. It is also a component of proteins, chlorophyll and nucleic acids. Nitrogen is easily washed out (leached) from the soil.

The way to spot nitrogen deficiency is if the plant has yellowing of the leaves known as chlorosis. This appears in the old leaves first. Another indication is if the growth of the plant is slow and spindly and the fruit and flowers are small. Plants such as brassicas, where the leafy green part is the bit that is eaten, require lots of nitrogen to grow well.

Phosphorus

P is the chemical symbol for phosphorus. This nutrient encourages root growth and also the ripening of fruit. It is a must for seed to germinate and it is recycled within the plant. It is important in the manufacture of proteins, enzymes and nucleic acid.

It is rare to find a deficiency in phosphorus, but the symptoms are leaves looking dull and falling ahead of time; they also may have a bluey-greenish tinge to them, and fruit and flowers are formed late and are often small.

Potassium

K is the symbol for potassium. Potassium is essential for fruiting and flowering. It also aids winter hardiness. If the soil is deficient in potassium you may have poor quality fruits and also find that leaves appear burnt and roll inwards and downwards.

Other nutrients

There are many other nutrients in soil, for example,

iron and manganese (which help with the production of chlorophyll), boron (which makes calcium available in a plant), and molybdenum (which helps plants to take up nitrogen).

If you are in doubt about the balance of nutrients in the soil in your allotment, it is possible to get the soil analysed. The kits you can buy for testing soil are generally to test for the three major nutrients of nitrogen, phosphorus and potassium, but there are companies that provide a soil analysis service. The RHS also offers this service. Usually, however, this won't be necessary as there are many ways to correct this and improve your soil yourself.

HOW TO IMPROVE THE SOIL

The best way to improve your soil, whether it be sandy or clay, is to add organic matter. This will improve the drainage on clay soils, and help the soil to heat up quicker. On sandy soils it will help to improve the structure of the soil and enable the soil to hold on to both water and nutrients for a longer period. Organic matter also provides some nutrients in its own right.

Green manures can also help to improve the soil. These are a group of plants, for example, clover (*Trifolium pratense*), mustard (*Sinapis alba*) and winter rye (*Secale cereale*), that are used to be grown in one season and then dug into the soil before they set seed or turn woody. Some of these plants, for example clover, have the ability to fix nitrogen in the soil.

Garden compost is another helpful medium that can be added to improve the soil.

FERTILIZERS

Plants are constantly taking nutrients from the soil and these need to be replaced in order to maintain a healthy soil. Soils need both bulky organic material in the form of compost or manure as well as nutrients in the form of fertilizers.

You have a choice either to have organic fertilizers which come directly from organic material, or inorganic fertilizers that are 'man made'.

Sometimes it is confusing when you are greeted with a huge range of fertilizers at the garden centre.

Comfrey can be used to make a 'tea' to feed your plants – and it's free!

Granular general fertilizer

This is a balanced general fertilizer and you will find an analysis written on the side of the bag – 7:7:7. This means that there is seven per cent each of nitrogen, phosphorus and potassium. If you prefer an organic fertilizer you should go for fish blood and bone meal instead. This is the best fertilizer to use before planting and sowing and it is usually applied two weeks before planting; if applied earlier it will either leach out of the soil, or burn the plants if applied too near planting time.

Liquid feed

This can give a 'gin and tonic' pick-me-up effect to a plant as it can get straight into the sap stream to give an instant boost. This can be used for general

Bark chippings used as a mulch can save hours of weeding.

feeding during the growing season; it is usually diluted and watered in.

Liquid tomato fertilizer

Don't be fooled - this is not just for tomatoes! It has a high potassium content and aids all fruiting and flowering plants as well as tomatoes. Again, this needs to be diluted and watered in.

Bone meal

Bone meal is a source of phosphorus, which aids root development. This is useful when planting bulbs, herbaceous perennials, shrubs, roses etc, as it helps the plant to establish itself. Bone meal is usually added in the autumn and should be sprinkled around the plant according to the manufacturer's instructions and then raked in. However, be warned – badgers and foxes love bone meal and will dig up plants if they can smell it.

Compost can be left to rot down in many different containers.

MULCHES

Mulching involves spreading 5–8cm (2–4in) of compost, manure, bark chippings etc, over the allotment and is a brilliant way of keeping weeds down. As long as it is put on thickly enough, it will stop weeds from germinating, then at the end of the season it can be dug into the soil to improve it. The best time to put it down is after a shower of rain; this will help to retain the moisture. Mulch also acts as a duvet on plants such as dahlias and cannas to help them overwinter.

Black polythene or membrane can be used as an effective mulch when planting strawberries, fruit bushes or hardwood cuttings. It is also a good idea to put down mulch when planting tomatoes, to suppress weeds and save lots of valuable time weeding at the busiest time of the year.

Mulch can also be put down on paths and a number of different materials can be used. It will often deter slugs and snails if something sharp such as chippings are used. Bark chippings are often available through local council or recycling areas. Do try to use a mulch – it saves hours of weeding and can look attractive as well.

DOS AND DON'TS OF COMPOST-MAKING

- Do not put weeds in your compost bin, otherwise you will end up with weeds growing all over your allotment.
- Don't put cooked food in the bin as this will attract rats.
- Do avoid using woody stems as they will take a long time to rot down.
- Do try to keep an even carbon/nitrogen mix; in other words, don't add too many grass clippings at once or this will cause the mixture to become slimy.
- Do add a bag of well-rotted manure to the contents of your bin to start the rotting-down process.

Taking out a trench a spit deep.

COMPOST

All gardeners have their own thoughts on how to make the best compost – here are mine! First of all, make sure the ground you stand the compost bin on is totally weed-free – you don't want compost full of ground elder or bindweed. You can easily make a bin out of old pallets, which are easy to get hold of, but make sure they are the non-returnable type. Make the front of your bin removable.

Start adding organic material such as vegetable peelings, tea leaves, egg shells, dead flowers, herbaceous material, torn-up newspaper, kitchen roll, lawn mowings and the soil from old growbags and flowerpots. Try to keep the compost heap covered with sacking to prevent it drying out or being soaked by rain. If the compost heap is well balanced there is no need to turn it and after six months you should have perfect compost that you can crumble in your hand and that does not smell. It is great to be able to spread the compost on your beds in the autumn to give your crops a good start and it is all recycled.

It's a good idea to have two bins, one to be filling

up while the other is full and rotting. If you have the space you could even make a third bin to put rotting leaves in; these take longer to decompose than compost and so they are best kept separate.

HOW TO DIG CORRECTLY

It will depend on what type of soil you have as to when you dig it. Clay is best dug early in the winter when the frost has broken down the clods of soil so that the ground can be raked. If you have to dig it at any other time, make sure that you do not dig it too deeply to allow for weathering to take place. On the other hand, sandy and chalky soils should be left until the last minute in the spring to avoid leaching of water and nutrients.

Before you start digging over your allotment, you need to make sure you have the correct-sized tool for the job. Make sure the spade is comfortable to hold and that it is the correct height for you; this will avoid putting unnecessary strain on your back.

Take it easy, don't rush to get it all done at once, and make sure you are using the right technique – this can make a whole lot of difference to your motivation. First of all take out a trench a spit deep (that's the depth of the spade), and take it to the back of the bed, then stand behind the first trench and add your organic matter. Next take out another trench behind the first one, turn over the soil and at the same time remove any perennial weeds and put them in a weed bucket. Put that soil on top of the first trench with the manure in it. Continue in this way until you reach the end and then add the first lot of soil dug from the first trench. This is a methodical way of working that allows you to see what you have dug; psychologically this is much more helpful than just digging randomly.

Remember that digging is strenuous exercise. Start by doing no more than half an hour a day and make sure not to put too much soil on your spade so it is too heavy to lift. If planned properly, digging need not be an onerous task. There is also a method called double-digging as opposed to single-digging described above. This is where you take out two spits deep of soil; however, this is really only necessary in extreme conditions where the subsoil needs breaking up.

CHAPTER 5

Vegetables – digging for your dinner

Most people want to grow vegetables on their allotments and there are plenty of good reasons to do so. Firstly, you know exactly what has gone into the soil; secondly, you can have the satisfaction of producing them yourself; and thirdly, you can grow and eat fresh produce in season. I like to grow lots of different varieties and this is perfectly possible with the many seed companies and organizations such as HDRA that have saved seeds of old varieties. You may also find there is a seed swap in your area where you can exchange seeds. Growing vegetables is also a way to increase your horticultural skills. Once you have been successful with one variety, try another!

Don't forget, however, that vegetables need food, water and good soil in order to grow well, so make sure you have time to prepare for them and give them what they need.

CROP ROTATION

The main reasons for crop rotation are to fight pests and disease, to preserve soil fertility and to maintain soil health. Years of experience have shown that if crops are rotated then yield will be higher and pests and diseases will be reduced. Crop rotation enables the life cycle of pests to be interrupted, thus disabling particular pests and diseases that favour particular conditions in which to thrive. Examples are white rot in onions, clubroot in brassicas and parsnip canker. If you continue to grow the same or related crops in the same place, this will provide the perfect home for its associated pests, bacteria or viruses.

Vegetables can look just as beautiful as flowers!

Soil fertility is another good reason for practising crop rotation. By meeting plants' nutritional needs you can help to maintain soil fertility; this can be done by taking into account the different needs of crops. For example, legumes, and in particular broad beans, have the ability to fix nitrogen in the soil from the atmosphere. Brassicas, on the other hand, need nitrogen to produce their green leafy growth and produce the flowers (the parts that we eat). Consequently it makes sense to grow brassicas after legumes. Root crops that need low nitrogen levels (root growth is promoted by phosphorus, a nutrient that is not usually deficient in the soil in Great Britain) can then follow on from the brassicas.

Rotating crops can also help to maintain the ideal soil pH. Legumes prefer a soil that has had organic matter added, which lowers the pH. Brassicas do better with a soil with a high pH (i.e. more alkaline) because clubroot does not like alkaline soil. Do not add manure and lime at the same time as they will have a chemical reaction to each other. The nitrogen will be lost as the two together speed up the breaking-down process.

It is also helpful to remember that certain plants perform different functions in controlling weeds and maintaining soil structure. For example, potatoes and other root vegetables help to break up the soil and keep it open. Potatoes also produce a large canopy of leaves and therefore suppress weeds, whereas onions are not good weed suppressers due to the nature of their vertical growth habit.

To enable crop rotation on your allotment, the creation of separate beds will help you. Beds may be flat, semi-flat or raised. A flat or semi-flat bed is simply marked out from the garden that surrounds it and cultivated. Every time this is done, and with

A climbing bean romping away in a soil with plenty of organic matter added.

organic matter and mulches added, the bed will gradually become raised above the path level. I prefer raised beds that are constructed by building the sides up to 30cm (12in) with timber, railway sleepers, bricks, cement or whatever is available to contain the soil. The crucial thing to remember is to have two complete cropping seasons without repeating a vegetable group if at all possible. Keeping a diary is a good way of ensuring that you remember where things have been planted. The main plant groups of legumes, brassicas and potatoes and root crops should be kept separate and other crops that you are growing can be placed in one group or another to suit other planting considerations. Sometimes it is more important to plant crops with those that share their cultivation requirements. For example, tomatoes are in the same family as potatoes, but they are not a root crop and they do not break up the soil, neither do they benefit from the nitrogen left by the brassicas, so they are best placed with the legumes instead.

Vegetables are usually grouped into categories because some are closely related and have similar cultivation requirements, which are different from other groups.

Permanent plants

These include asparagus, artichokes (both globe and Jerusalem varieties) and rhubarb, which is also classed as a vegetable. Most vegetables are grown as annuals but the permanent plants are grown as perennials because they come back each year. These plants are all very attractive and can look wonderful planted together in a permanent bed.

Brassicas

This family (*Brassicaceae*) is the largest in the vegetable garden. Brassicas include cabbage, cauliflower, broccoli, Brussels sprouts, and also, much to most people's surprise, swedes and turnips. The family also includes radish, rocket, mizuna and other leafy oriental vegetables.

Crop rotation is very important for this group of plants, as they are very vulnerable to the unrelenting soil-borne disease clubroot. This family also suffers from serious pests such as cabbage root fly and caterpillars, and these need to be controlled. Clubroot can remain active in the soil for up to twenty years and consequently crop rotation is essential to prevent build-up of this fungal disease.

Legumes

Legumes include all the beans and peas. The family name is *Leguminosae*, which means pod-bearing. All legumes are grown as annual crops. Broad beans and peas are crops that are resistant to frost and are adapted to cool climates. However, others such as runner beans and French beans thrive best in warm areas and are grown as half-hardy annuals. These plants have the ability to fix nitrogen in the soil from the air and, with the help of nodules on their roots, consequently need less nitrogen fertilizer than other crops. Their roots can be dug back into the soil after harvesting to provide nitrogen for the brassica crop. They grow best in full sun and they prefer a sheltered position. They are hungry plants and so need a rich soil.

GUIDE TO VEGETABLE YIELDS

The following yields are for a row 2m (6ft) long.

VEGETABLE	YIELD
Bean, runner	12kg (26lb)
Bean, French	3kg (6lb)
Beetroot	5kg (10lb)
Broccoli (sprouting)	2kg (4lb)
Brussels sprout	4kg (9lb)
Cabbage	6kg (13lb)
Carrot	6kg (13lb)
Cauliflower	4kg (9lb)
Celery	3kg (6lb)
Chinese cabbage	3kg (6lb)
Courgette	6kg (13lb)
Leek	6kg (13lb)
Lettuce	2kg (4lb)
Onion, bulb	5kg (10lb)
Parsnip	6kg (13lb)
Pea	4kg (9lb)
Potato	8kg (18lb)
Squash	8kg (18lb)
Spinach	2kg (4lb)
Swede	4kg (9lb)
Sweet corn	2kg (4lb)
Tomato	6kg (13lb)
Turnip	4kg (9lb)

Alliums

These are the bulbs of the *Alliacaea* family, and include onions, leeks, garlic and shallots. If you are careful, you can choose cultivars so that you can eat them almost all year round. They are best grown in an open site so that the humidity that encourages disease can be avoided. Although they like manured soil, it is important not to plant them into freshly-manured ground as the plants are likely to grow too 'soft' and will be more likely to develop disease. I prefer to grow from onion sets, as they are less prone to disease. They are also easier to look after as onion seed will require a lot more work in their early life. Sets are also less likely to get onion fly and will tolerate poor soils.

Root crops

In this group you will find plants with swollen tap roots such as beetroot, parsnips and carrots, as well as Hamburg parsley, salsify and scorzonera. Most of these crops store well and are useful over winter. Again, with these crops rotation is important, as they are prone to pests and diseases such as eel-worm and parsnip canker.

Root crops all have different requirements as far as nutrients are concerned. Carrots and beet have very low nitrogen requirements but all crops do best on soils with a lot of added organic matter. However, this is best added into the soil at least six months before planting.

SPACING

Spacing of crops is something everyone seems to get confused with. It really is best to try to devise your own measuring system – for example, spacing plants 10cm, 4in or a hand-span apart. My own preference is to use the measurement of a thumb-nail for 2cm or 1in. A boot is another good way of measuring a foot, 12in or 30cm. That way if you don't have anything with you at your allotment to measure your planting distances, you will soon get used to your own way of doing it. It also makes it easier to visualize distances.

A-Z OF VEGETABLES

Asparagus: Asparagus officinalis

Life cycle: Perennial.
Site and soil: Good drainage is essential and a pH of 6.3–7.5 is essential for asparagus to thrive. Rich and weed-free soil is important. Asparagus is best grown in traditional raised beds.
Plant: One-year-old crowns in April, or if you are patient grow from seed in April.
Planting distance: Single rows 30cm (1ft) apart in the base of a trench, or alternatively plant two rows 30cm (1ft) apart and leave 1m (3ft) between each of the double rows to create a 'bed'.
Time before harvesting: You can cut your asparagus from late April to late June in the third season onwards.

The ferns of an asparagus plant can be used in flower arranging.

How many? Nine to ten spears per crown from mature plants.

Asparagus is a luxury and because of this well worth growing. When my father was a child, nearly ninety years ago, his father would send him and his brothers and sisters out to look for any old iron such as old bedsprings and the like to put into the bottom of the asparagus trench to presumably add iron to the soil! Luckily those days have gone and gardeners today can rely on manure and garden compost to get good results. Asparagus is an unusual crop in that it produces both male and female plants; the male plants produce more spears. The problem with the female plants is that they tend to self-seed everywhere, but you can buy hybrids that produce only male plants. In any case

they are a very classy vegetable – their foliage is very beautiful as well and can be used in flower arranging.

Varieties

'Franklim' is a good variety as it is a hybrid all-male plant and crops heavily. 'Regal' is another good choice and seems to do well in trials.

Site and soil

Firstly, be sure to avoid frost pockets as they can damage the new spears early on in the season. Make sure your asparagus plants are grown on a sheltered site as the wind can snap off the ferny foliage, which in turn stops the food from getting to the crown of the plant where it is stored. The other thing to watch for is that the crowns, which are fleshy, tend to rot if the soil is not well-drained. This is why it is best to grow them in a raised bed with plenty of organic matter added to improve drainage.

Seed sowing

If you are very patient, then grow your asparagus from seed. It is very easy to grow from seed but it will hold up the already lengthy process of waiting for your crop. You can sow them in April in pots under glass and you will soon have some plants. However, you will need to wait for a whole year before they are ready to plant out. It is a good idea, if you enjoy growing things from seed, to have some at the ready in case you lose some of your crowns.

Planting

Crowns are one-year-old plants, and they look a lot like shrunken dahlia tubers. Try to plant them as soon as possible after you get them to stop them dehydrating. If you are unable to plant them straight away, wrap them up in wet newspaper. Don't forget that asparagus is a very long-term crop, often cropping for up to twenty-five years. So think carefully about the position of your beds as they may well be there for a very long time!

Space your crowns 30cm (1ft) apart each way; that way you can have three rows to a bed. April is the best time to plant them. Make sure you prepare the bed well. Dig a trench for each row 15cm (6in) deep and carefully spread out the crowns. They are very fragile, so treat them with care. Then cover them with 7.5cm (3in) of soil. Finally give them a really good water. They will not stand drying out.

Cultivation

In the first year it is imperative that you do not let your crop dry out. Give the plants a liquid feed at monthly intervals in the first year. In the autumn, when the foliage turns yellow (but before the fruit ripens and falls), cut the plant down to 2.5cm (1in) above the ground and cover it with some well-rotted manure.

In the second year, give your plants some general-purpose fertilizer, such as blood, fish and bone, in the spring before the shoots can be seen. Keep the bed weed-free and if need be stake the foliage to stop it falling over. In the autumn, cut down the foliage as before.

In the third spring, keep feeding the soil and then hopefully in April it will all have been worth it as you will have a crop!

Harvesting

The asparagus can be cut from late April to late June from the third season onwards. You can get a special asparagus knife with a serrated blade, which you may wish to invest in after all the trouble of growing the plants! Failing that, of course, you can use an old kitchen knife. Make sure that you cut every spear, even those that are thin; they will all be tasty, and cutting them all is necessary to stimulate the dormant buds to produce next year's spears. The thin spears are knows as a 'spruce' and the wonky ones known as 'crooks'. Give the plants a feed after picking to give them a boost for next year.

The spears will keep for about a week in the fridge and of course you can freeze them if you want some for a special occasion.

Common problems

As usual, watch out for slugs as they nibble the plants. The worst pest is the asparagus beetle because both adults and larvae cause damage. Watch out for the adults in the spring; they have black and white wing cases and a red under-body. The larvae are dark grey in colour and look like caterpillars. Pick them off and check for them among the dense foliage. The best thing to do is to burn the foliage and then you will make sure the beetles and their larvae have been destroyed.

Beetroot: Beta vulgaris

Life cycle: Hardy biennial grown as an annual.
Site and soil: Tolerant of most types of soil. Prefers sun or partial shade.
Sow: Sow under cover using bolt-resistant cultivars in spring and then make successional sowing outside every two weeks in early and mid-summer.
Time before harvesting: Ten weeks for common round types and eighteen weeks for long types.
How many? Twelve round types per metre, or six long types per metre.

Beetroot is a very versatile vegetable – you can eat it hot or pickle it and it is lovely grated raw in salads. You can even make wine with it as it has a high sugar content. Wild beetroot was originally

The leaves of the young beetroot can be used in salads.

gathered for its leaves, which can be eaten in salads. In ancient times, beetroot was believed to promote good blood because of its colour.

Varieties

'Bolthardy' is a round globe variety and is highly recommended as it does not run to seed and has a good colour. 'Burpee's golden' is a good-tasting Victorian type of beetroot. The leaves are good for eating too. 'Bull's Blood' is good to grow for its fantastic red leaves and great taste.

Site and soil

Beetroot needs an open, sunny site, with fertile, light, sandy soil, best manured in the previous season. As with other root vegetables, the long-rooted varieties need a deep soil and a pH of 6.5–7 if possible.

Sowing and planting

It is possible to grow beetroot in modules and carefully transplant them, but you must take great care when planting them that you do not snap the roots. For spring beet grown under cover, make sure you use a bolt-resistant variety. You can sow them every two weeks in early and mid-summer, about 5cm (2in) apart. You can help the seeds to germinate by soaking them overnight.

Cultivation

Protect the early sowings from frost. They are easy to grow and relatively trouble-free. Keep the plants weeded and water them to prevent wood roots or splitting caused by irregular watering.

Harvesting

You can lift the beetroots when they are about the size of a tennis ball; after that they begin to get woody. You can have 'baby' beet when they are the size of a golf ball. Be careful not to damage the roots when lifting them. Harvest them by pulling up the beets and twisting off their tops. They can be left in the ground or put in a clamp as for carrots and parsnips.

Common problems

Blackfly may attack the leaves or cutworms may be a problem. Occasionally the beetroot plants may show deficiencies of boron (rough, cankered patches on the roots with rotting at the heart) and manganese (yellowing between the leaf veins, and interveinal chlorosis of older leaves).

Broad beans: *Vicia fabia*

Life cycle: Hardy annual.
Site and soil: Any reasonable soil, preferably in full sun.
Sow: October to December or February to June.
Time before harvesting: Fourteen weeks.
Harvest: June to September.
How many? Average of 5kg (11lb) for each 3m (10ft) row.

Broad beans are really easy plants to grow, great for the beginner and expert alike. Some varieties produce beautiful flowers and can be grown in the flower border and also in containers. They are very nutritious, high in riboflavin and vitamin C and also a good source of protein. The Ancient Egyptians believed that when a person died his soul temporarily lived in the broad bean prior to passing on to the next life.

Varieties

'Red Epicure' is an unusual variety with lovely, rich crimson seed. Although not a heavy cropper, it produces coloured beans that unfortunately lose their colour on cooking. The other variety to try if you want unusual flowers is the crimson-flowered variety. However, although this looks fantastic, you won't be able to feed a lot of people on it as it does not produce many beans.

For a more reliable crop, sow 'Aquadulce Claudia' between October and December. This variety is very hardy and early-maturing. 'Sutton' is hard to beat as it is dwarf and produces well, so is good for small areas.

Site and soil

An area that is in full sun and that has had well-rotted manure or garden compost added is best for broad beans. It is best to dig over the soil and add the manure or compost in late summer for the autumn sowings or in the autumn for the spring sowings. I always throw in a couple of handfuls of fertilizer for good measure about two weeks before planting. You may need to lime the soil in winter if it is acid.

Seed sowing

If you sow your beans in the autumn, make sure they are the hardy types suitable for this time of year. It is a good idea to sow some 'Aquadulce Claudia' in about November and then put some extras in pots in the cold frame or greenhouse to fill in if it does get cold in the winter and some get damaged. Always make sure that you use a cane or preferably a line to mark out where your rows are; even the best eye can get it wrong and then hoeing is very difficult.

Mark up a plank with measurements on it and then you can kneel on it at the same time. Broad beans need to be sown about 5cm (2in) deep, and at about 15cm (6in) intervals. Simply push the seed down and cover it over with your hand. Make another row about 23cm (9in) away; this is so you have a double row. You should then leave 60cm (2ft) between the rows.

If you want you can plant them out in the cold frame in pots in January and then transfer them to their final position in March. It is still necessary to use a cloche in the really cold weather to give them a bit of protection and at the same time reduce the chance of them being eaten.

Cultivation

Remove the cloches when the weather improves so that air can get to the plants.

As with all vegetables, keep them weed-free and well watered, especially when it is very dry. When four or five flower clusters have appeared, pinch out the top. This will encourage the pods to swell and also prevent the blackfly from attacking them, as they seem to prefer the tender tips. Assuming they are not swarming in aphids, you can eat the tops raw in salads.

It is best to stake the taller varieties of bean by putting canes at intervals throughout the crop and then threading string through and tying it to the canes, incorporating each individual bean plant.

Harvesting

When you can see the beans showing through the

Broad beans should have their growing tops pinched out (these can then be eaten in a salad) to avoid attack from blackfly.

pods, pick them regularly. Use scissors to snip them off so that they don't get damaged. Make sure they do not get too old as they become inedible.

Common problems

Chocolate spot and rust are two common fungal diseases that broad beans can suffer from. Chocolate spot is worse when the weather is damp and humid early on in the season and rust seems to be more of a problem when there are dry periods. Although they look unsightly they will not affect the beans' taste. Blackfly and pea and bean weevil are also a problem; if they should attack, cover the plants with horticultural fleece or pinch out the tops.

Broccoli and calabrese: Brassica oleracea (Italica group)

Life cycle: Half-hardy perennial grown as an annual in the UK.

Site and soil: Sunny site and firm, fairly rich soil that is not too acid.

Sow: April and May for broccoli; April to June for calabrese.

Plant: June to August.

Planting distance: 30cm (12in) between calabrese plants, and 45cm (18in) between purple and white sprouting plants and rows.

Time before harvesting: Fifteen to forty weeks, depending on the variety.

How many? Calabrese 1kg (2.2lb) per plant. Other varieties vary.

The word broccoli means 'little sprouts' in Italian. The Romans were enamoured with broccoli and Pliny the Elder, the Italian naturalist and writer, said that the Romans grew and enjoyed broccoli as early as the first century CE. It became a standard favourite in Rome where the variety called calabrese was developed. There is some confusion about the difference between broccoli and calabrese; the basic difference is that purple and white sprouting broccoli matures in late winter and spring, whereas calabrese (the name given to the green sprouting kind) is not winter-hardy and matures in the later summer and early autumn. Early purple and late white will give you a succession of heads on your winter crop.

Varieties

'Arcadia' (calabrese) has a firm head and is both quick-maturing and very reliable. 'Green Comet' (calabrese) is a quick-maturing F1 hybrid (the first generation of plants from pure-bred parents). The green heads are large and tightly formed. Early purple sprouting broccoli is a hardy and prolific variety producing purple heads that can be harvested from mid-March, and late white sprouting broccoli is another hardy and prolific cropper, producing heads like small cauliflower.

Site and soil

Site and soil is mostly the same as for other brassicas. Trample the soil in winter to make sure it is firm and then apply the usual rules; apply lime and organic matter or garden compost as necessary.

Seed sowing

Because of the large differences in sowing to harvest times for different types of broccoli, it is extra-important to examine the instructions on the seed packets. That way you won't pick the wrong variety! They can be sown directly into the soil but are generally best started off in modules; this way they are more likely to survive. Plant them out when they are about 10cm (4in) high – the lowest leaves should be just above soil level. Sow calabrese outdoors in early May or indoors earlier in April and then plant them out in May. Purple broccoli seeds can be sown in late April and the white variety in early May.

Cultivation

As the plants develop, water them well so that they form good flower heads. Hoe off weeds around them and in July hoe in a little general fertilizer along the rows to give them a boost.

Harvesting

Cut the central flower head from calabrese as soon as it is 18cm (3in) across; this will allow the plant to form side-shoots, which will produce smaller heads. These can be harvested before the autumn frosts. Purple and white sprouting broccoli can be picked when ready from late February onwards. If you keep picking them they will produce more shoots.

Common problems

These are much the same as with other brassicas. Try tying some old CDs above your plants, as this can help deter the pigeons.

Brussels sprouts: Brassica oleracea

Life cycle: Hardy biennial grown as an annual.

Site and soil: An open, sunny site that has rich, firm well-drained soil that is not too acid.

Sow: February under cloches or in a cold frame, or March to April in the open ground.

Plant: April to June (seedlings).

Planting distance: 76cm (30in) between the plants and the rows.

Time before harvesting: thirty-two weeks.

How many? 1kg (2.2lbs) per plant.

Brussels sprouts are fantastic! They are a marvellous winter standby and are a real delight, especially after a frost. It is possible to enjoy them from early autumn to spring.

Varieties

'Rubine' is an old variety with a beautiful crimson colour and a great nutty taste. 'Maximus AGM' has high yields of medium-sized sprouts that are mid-green and give some resistance to powdery mildew.

Site and soil

They prefer an open sunny site with plenty of organic matter dug into the soil in the autumn or winter before sowing. During the winter time, dust with lime if the soil is acid. Trample the soil in the spring to make sure that the ground is really firm; if not, the plants will topple over. A week or two before planting, add a couple of handfuls of general-purpose fertilizer over each square metre of ground and rake it in.

Seed sowing

The earliest sowings can be made in a cold greenhouse in February. You can sow them outside from March to April, but I find they get eaten so it is better to grow them under glass to start them off.

Planting

Plant them outside in May or June, leaving at least 76cm (30in) between plants to allow the air to circulate around them. Young plants should be supported with a stake to ensure they grow straight; if not they may develop a kink and not stand upright. You might want to use a sweet pea ring with a small green cane to start your sprouts off.

Cultivation

Make sure that you keep your plants weed-free and pull up some soil around the stems about a month after planting. Keep them well watered in dry weather. In midsummer give them a feed with a high potash food such as the one you use on your tomatoes, or you could give them some pelleted chicken manure. In autumn pull off any lower leaves that have turned yellow. They will need to be supported on windy sites with a cane for each plant; tie this at the top of the stem.

Brussels sprouts are a good winter crop.

Harvesting

When the sprouts are about the size of a walnut, snap them cleanly from the stem. Start at the bottom and work upwards.

Common problems

Protect plants against cabbage root fly by making collars to put around the base of your plant so that the female cannot lay her eggs on the plant. Pigeons, caterpillars, and cabbage white butterflies can cause many problems. To prevent pests it is best to grow your brassicas under netting from the beginning. Make sure the netting is very fine to stop pests getting through the holes. To be sure to stop pests, construct a permanent frame around the plants as when they mature it is difficult to net them. Clubroot and mildew are also a problem. Make sure that you give the plants plenty of space, lime the soil if it is acid and practise crop rotation to help avoid these diseases.

Cabbage: *Brassica oleracea (Capitata group)*

Life cycle: Half-hardy perennial vegetable grown as an annual in the UK.
Site and soil: Cabbages like fertile, well-drained, firm, moisture-retentive soil.
Sow: Spring cabbages in summer; autumn cabbages in spring and winter cabbages in early summer. Red cabbages are sown in spring.
Planting distance: Allow 30–45cm (12–18in) in between plants, depending on the size of the variety.
Time before harvesting: Twenty to thirty-five weeks, depending on the variety.
How many? This depends on variety as they can vary considerably in size.

Cabbages seem to have got themselves a very bad reputation – possibly from most of us that ate them boiled to death and cold with our school dinners. However, they really are great plants and look wonderful in the vegetable plot – and of course it is possible to harvest them all year round.

Varieties

For spring, 'Durham Elf' is good, as is 'Pixie', which is an early variety that is also good for spring greens and successional or summer sowing. For summer, try 'Hispi' – an old favourite with a pointed head. 'Derby Day' is another old favourite and this one has a round head. Summer/autumn varieties include 'Quickstep' which can cope well with the hot weather. 'Kilaxy' also deserves a mention as it is said to be resistant to clubroot and is very tasty, with firm and compact heads.

Among the winter cabbage varieties, 'Holly' is an easy name to remember and this is a January King type with purple heads. 'Protovoy' is a Savoy type of cabbage. For red cabbage, choose between 'Rookie', which is great in salads but does not store well, or 'Rodeo', which again does not store well but is ready for harvest in late summer.

Site and soil

The cabbage prefers a soil that is fertile, well-drained and moisture-retentive. As for all brassicas, soil needs to be firm, so on planting do the tug test – give the plant a tug when it is planted to make sure it doesn't move out of the soil. Lime the soil if necessary to raise the pH to guard against clubroot. Liming will not only raise the pH but will provide calcium and encourage worms and the bacteria population. It will also aid a process called flocculation, which enables the small clay particles to bind together, making the soil more workable.

Seed sowing and planting

It is possible to grow cabbages to mature all year round and the sowing dates vary according to when the cabbages are to be harvested. Sow early summer varieties under cloches, or in a cold frame or glasshouse in late winter or early spring, and transplant them into their final positions in mid-spring. Sow your main summer season cabbages in modules in mid-spring and plant them out in late spring and early summer.

For cabbages to cut from late summer through into autumn, sow them in modules from mid-spring to mid-summer and plant them out from early to late summer. If you want winter varieties, sow these between mid-spring and mid-summer, but of course this will depend on the variety. They can then be planted out in mid–late summer. Sow your spring cabbages in mid–late summer and plant them out in early to mid-autumn; they can then overwinter and provide you with spring greens in the early spring. If you leave them, they will form firm heads a few weeks later. One thing is for sure – you can be kept very busy sowing cabbages!

Cultivation

Keep your cabbages weed-free and make sure you water them really well by puddling them in when you transplant them. Give them a really good watering during dry spells, but otherwise they can survive well, needing little water, except when they are beginning to form hearts, when extra water will improve their size.

Harvesting

Cut the heads when they are ready and place any unwanted leaves on the compost heap.

Common problems

Aphids, flea beetle, cabbage root fly, caterpillars, cabbage whitefly and pigeons are all pests and the best way to defend against all these is to net your plants with very fine netting at the time of transplanting, or erect a 'fruit cage'. As usual with brassicas, clubroot can be a serious problem so take the necessary precautions.

Carrots: Daucus carota

Life cycle: Biennial.
Site and soil: Open, sunny site with well-drained fertile soil. Make sure it is not freshly manured.
Sow: March under cloches and April to July outdoors.
Harvest: June to October.
Time before harvesting: Twelve to fifteen weeks (June to October).
How many? 6kg (13lb) in a two-metre row.

There's a saying that 'It's all in the soil' and in the case of carrots that is true. Loose, even soil is essential as carrots are quite difficult to grow well unless you have the perfect conditions. Maincrop varieties, which can be stored for up to three months, make it possible to have a near year-round supply. The tastiest carrots are the early varieties, which can be harvested as early as May when they are at their most expensive in the shops. They are a good vegetable for the beginner, but make sure you read all about their requirements first!

Carrots are rich in vitamin A, calcium and trace elements and a good source of fibre.

Varieties

The best early variety to grow under cloches is 'Adelaide' as this makes an excellent early crop. Furthermore, the fact that it is stump-ended at its roots makes it easier to penetrate to soil. If you have a stony or shallow soil or want to grow carrots in containers, try 'Parmex', which are round-rooted carrots. 'Flyaway' is a main crop variety with a good resistance to carrot fly.

Site and soil

The best soil for carrots is a light, sandy soil in which there are no stones. However, not many peo-

Growing carrots in a drainpipe or similar is a way of combating poor or thin soil.

ple are lucky enough to have this, so try to produce a good soil suitable for them by deeply digging the ground in winter and raking it to a fine tilth in spring. Try to remove any stones that will cause the roots to fork. Don't add manure as this will give you lots of lovely lush tops and not much in the way of anything to eat. Two weeks before you sow your carrots, feed the soil with fish, blood and bone or similar.

Sowing

Sow the first crop in late winter or early spring under a cloche or cold frame. You can begin to sow outdoors from early spring, sowing half way across the plot and then two weeks later sowing some more. You must try and avoid having to thin them so sow thinly. The carrot fly, which is a major pest, will be attracted to the smell when you thin them.

STORAGE IN CLAMPS

To store using the clamp method, the first thing to ensure is that the crop will be kept out of standing water. Choose a dry spot, then dig a trench around the storage area. This will help drain any water and will also provide the soil you will need later. Next place a layer of straw, bracken or even shredded paper on the ground and then place a layer of your crop down. With carrots, you could try a wheel-spoke pattern, with the thick end of the carrots to the outside of the circle. Then place another layer of sand or cardboard over the crop. Carry on adding layers to form a cone shape. On the outside of the clamp, place six to eight inches of straw and make a little straw spike at the top. This will allow excess moisture to escape. The soil you removed from your drainage trench can then be used to cover the clamp.

Companion planting can help with reducing the damage of the carrot fly; try planting them with spring onions or something that smells strongly to confuse the carrot fly. You can also avoid the fly by sowing the main crop in June as the prime danger period is May when the flies are the most common.

Cultivation

Carrots are a drought-resistant crop and enjoy the hot weather but make sure they do not dry out as they will often split. Keep the area around them weed-free.

Harvesting

Carrots are generally ready for harvesting twelve to sixteen weeks after sowing, but you can have young carrots earlier. Make sure you use a fork when lifting them to avoid damaging them. If you want to store them, leave them in the ground for the full time. Carrots are best kept in the soil, but if you should need to lift them because the soil is wet, store them stacked in a polystyrene box or similar filled with sand.

In the days when people had large families and often survived by what they grew for themselves, it was common to store root crops such as potatoes, carrots, swedes, beetroot and celeriac in clamps. Traditionally carrots are stored in a clamp, which is a conical-shaped mound of straw and sand in which vegetables are layered, but they are probably not the best method for storing the smaller amounts required by a small family or couple.

Common problems

The most common problem with carrots is the carrot fly, and there are various ways of keeping it at bay, such as companion planting, sowing thinly and keeping the main crop sowing to June. It is also worth surrounding your carrots with a 50cm (20in) barrier made of horticultural fleece, stapled to some stakes, to keep the carrot fly away; the carrot fly generally flies close to the ground so this barrier will confuse it and keep it away.

Cauliflower: Brassica Oleracea Botrytis

Life cycle: Annual.
Site and soil: All cauliflowers need a neutral or slightly alkaline soil to do well.
Plant: March to May for summer varieties; June and July for autumn and winter varieties.
Planting distance: 38–60cm (15–24in) apart; 60–90cm (24–36in) between rows.
Time before harvesting: Eighteen to twenty-four weeks for summer cauliflower, and thirty-six to thirty-eight weeks for winter cauliflower.
Yield and size: The yield is 0.5–1.0kg (1–2lb) per plant, with five to seven plants per 3m (10ft) row. Heads are 10–37.5cm (4–15in) across, stalks 7.5–15 cm (3–6in) long, leaves 45–60cm (18–24in) high.
How many? Five to six large ones in a 3m (10ft) row or twenty mini-cauliflowers in the same row.

The cauliflower is an annual from the north-east Mediterranean. They are quite difficult to grow as they can be damaged by hard frost and require lots of water, more than is usually provided by the summer rains; consequently it is better to grow cultivars that come to maturity before mid-summer. The typical cauliflower produces white curds or heads but you can also get green- or purple-headed varieties. They are large plants and those that overwinter will be in the ground for almost a year. But

Cauliflowers require a lot of water.

despite all this, cauliflowers are beautiful vegetables with their green leaves and contrasting white curds and being able to grow some is a real triumph!

Varieties

Among the summer cauliflowers, 'Fargo' matures in early summer. 'Idol' is a good variety for a mini-cauliflower. Among the winter varieties, 'Ondine' is good as it will stand a light frost. 'White Dove' is a hybrid that matures in late winter. Among the spring varieties, 'Patriot' gives good leaf protection and 'Mayfair' is a good hybrid for late spring.

Site and soil

Pick a sunny and sheltered site for your cauliflowers, making sure to avoid frost pockets for the winter varieties. This is where crop rotation really comes in as brassicas benefit from being planted after legumes which fix the nitrogen necessary for cauliflowers etc. to develop. Dig the soil well and add well-rotted garden compost or manure, as much as you can get, as cauliflowers will not grow if the soil is dry. Ensure that the soil is firm as cauliflowers, like all brassicas, must have a firm soil to prevent them from falling over.

Seed sowing

There are three ways of sowing summer cauliflowers. You can sow them in 1cm (½ in) deep drills 23cm (9in) apart in an outdoor seedbed in late September and then transplant them to 10cm (4in) apart under cloches or into a cold frame the follow-ing month. Then in the following March or April they can be transplanted into their final positions. I prefer to sow them in a heated greenhouse in February, harden them off and plant them out in April. If you have no crop protection for them, then sow them outdoors in March and April.

For autumn and winter types, sow them outdoors in April and May. I always raise my seedlings in module trays as this makes it much easier when it comes to planting them out. I do this when they are 8–10 cm (3–4in) high. Make sure you water the bed thoroughly before planting and plant them with a trowel, puddling them in with a watering can or hosepipe.

Plant summer varieties 45cm (18in) apart and allow 60cm (2ft) between the rows. The autumn and winter types will make larger plants, so allow 60cm (2ft) between them and 75cm (2½ft) between the rows.

Cultivation

Make sure the rows are kept weed-free and keep the plants well watered in dry periods. You should protect your cauliflowers from direct sunlight and frost by bending over one of two of the inner leaves; this will shelter the developing curd.

Harvesting

Cut the curds while they are still small, making sure that the flowers do not begin to separate. Cut through the stem with a sharp knife. Keep some leaves around the cauliflower to protect it. You can compost the rest of the leaves and stem.

Common problems

The usual problems with brassicas occur and also watch out for loose curds or any going to flower too early. This may mean the ground is not firm enough, or that they have not had sufficient water or that the soil is not rich enough.

Courgette: *Curcubita pepo*

Life cycle: Half-hardy annual.
Site and soil: Rich soil with good drainage in full sun.
Time before harvesting: Twelve to fourteen weeks.

How many? On average, fifteen courgettes per plant.

Courgettes are very easy plants to grow and very rewarding as they will provide you with lots of fruits to make summer dishes from and also to use in pickles. If you leave them on the plant for too long they will turn into marrows (botanically courgettes are the same as marrows – they just mature into larger fruits). Courgettes are seedless as they are eaten when they are young. They can be grown on a compost heap; the conditions of the compost heap, as long as it is kept watered, are ideal.

Varieties

'Bambino' is an early fruiting variety with dark green fruits. 'Black Forest' is a climbing variety that is good for small spaces as it can be trained over a trellis or arch. 'Jemmer' is a compact variety with prolific yellow fruits and 'Rondo di Nice' has round fruits if you want to experiment with something different.

Site and soil

Courgettes prefer an open sunny position and must have plenty of organic matter incorporated into the soil before planting as they are hungry plants.

Sowing and planting

It is best to start courgettes off in the greenhouse in late spring and plant them outdoors in the early summer. They will not tolerate frost and as they grow quickly there is no need to sow them any earlier than a month before the last predicted frost. Sow two seeds into a pot and when they have produced their first true leaves (the ones that look like courgette leaves), throw away or try to pot on the weakest ones. I always keep a few back in case the others get eaten. They do need a lot of space and so they need 90cm (36in) between the rows and the plants.

Cultivation

These plants guzzle up loads of water and so keep them near your water supply. Make sure the soil is kept moist, especially during flowering. Keep the area weed-free. Trailing types need training over arches or frames.

The courgette flower is edible as well as the fruit.

If the summer is cool, you may notice that the fruit is not setting, which is probably because there are not enough pollinators, so they may need some help. You can remove a male flower and brush the central parts against the centre of a female flower. You can tell a female flower as you can feel the ovary behind the flower head.

Harvesting

Courgettes seem to grow before your very eyes – one day there are none, and the next you may have several. Try to harvest them when they are about 10cm (4in) long. Use a sharp knife and gloves as they are quite spiny plants. Don't try to pull them off as you can damage the plant and prevent further fruiting.

Common problems

Powdery mildew can occur in the late summer and cucumber mosaic virus is common but the best

This garlic has been smoked and consequently can be kept for several months.

thing to do is to buy disease-resistant cultivars. Red spider mite and whitefly only seem to occur if the plants are in cold frames.

Garlic: Allium sativum

Life cycle: Annual bulb.
Site and soil: Garlic needs a sunny site to ripen the bulbs, with well-drained soil.
Time before harvesting: ten months.
How many? Seventeen bulbs per 3m (10ft) row.

Garlic has always been a much-valued plant; medicinal prescriptions for garlic were found carved into a clay tablet that was more than 3,000 years old. It is the key ingredient to a wide variety of recipes and is said to cure over sixty ailments, according the Pliny the Elder. Its medicinal properties were said to aid athletes before they took part in the Olympics in Ancient Greece. Moreover, it is easy to grow given the correct soil and planting time – so do give it a go.

Varieties
'White Pearl' is good for autumn or winter planting as it is ninety-five per cent virus-free, and tends not to suffer from either white rot or attack by eel-worms. Try 'Novatop' with white skin, which is also virus-free, and 'Sultop', which has pink cloves that can be planted in the spring.

Site and soil
Garlic needs full sun as it needs to grow quickly in order to produce good sized bulbs. It also needs a cold period of one or two months, so it is best to plant it before Christmas. Well drained, light, alkaline soil is best and if you have a heavy soil it should be given some horticultural sand to lighten it. Avoid using fresh manure, as this may cause the bulbs to rot, but dig in some well-rotted manure well before planting.

Planting
You can start your garlic seedlings off in modules and plant them out later on if the soil is too wet.

Globe artichokes are a permanent crop and look great underplanted with allium.

Plant them 10cm (4in) deep and the same apart, with 45cm (18in) between the rows. Grow your garlic from cloves, which you can break away from the bulb as you would if using for cooking. Make sure you have the basal plate as the end going into the soil (the basal plate is where the roots are formed) and add a couple of handfuls of bone meal at planting time to help the cloves set down roots.

Cultivation

Keep the garlic plants weed-free and moist to avoid growth slowing down. You can plant them through black plastic to keep the plants warm and also retain moisture and suppress weeds as, like onions, they have little foliage to do the job themselves. Garlic is also suitable for intercropping.

Harvesting

Lift autumn- or winter-planted varieties in late spring or early summer as soon as their leaves start to fade and turn yellow. Spring-planted garlic should be harvested from midsummer to early autumn. You can plait your garlic together and hang it up in a dry place; stored like this, it will keep for several months.

Common problems

Garlic can suffer from the same diseases as bulb onions. Viruses can also be a problem, so buy your garlic from a reputable company rather than using the garlic in your larder.

Globe artichoke: *Cyanara scolymus*

Life cycle: Perennial.
Site and soil: A sunny and sheltered site with well-drained moisture-retentive soil.
Sow: Late winter to early spring under glass.
Plant: In early summer.

Planting distance: 1m (3ft) each way.
Time before harvesting: Although they will produce flowers in the first year it is better to wait until the second year for them to establish before harvesting.
How many? Each mature plant should produce at least ten fat flower heads each year.

The globe artichoke is such a handsome plant, I always think it looks too good to eat, with its majestic silver leaves and thistle-like flower heads. However, I usually give in as this plant, although very welcome in the flower border, is absolutely delicious to eat. Do grow some on your allotment – they really are a worthwhile plant for looks and taste.

Varieties
'Green Globe' is a popular variety and can be grown from seed, but if possible it is better to obtain some suckers from a friend's plants, as sometimes plants raised from seed can produce scrawny flower heads. Suckers from such plants as 'Violetta di Chioggia' give much more reliable plants and produce great-tasting purple heads.

Site and soil
A sunny and sheltered site is essential as these plants are not fully hardy. They are extremely greedy, so add plenty of well-rotted manure to the planting site, at least two bucketfuls to each square metre, and add horticultural grit to clay soils to improve drainage. Rake in some general-purpose fertilizer just before planting – something like fish, blood and bone or pelleted chicken manure will work well.

Seed-sowing
Rather than sow seed, it is much better to obtain suckers from high-yielding parents, so ask among other allotmenteers. If this is not possible, sow seed at 15°C (59°F) in late winter to early spring in 9cm (3in) pots, one seed to a pot. Harden off the seedlings gradually and plant out in early summer.

Planting
Make sure you give your plants plenty of space, 1m (3ft) in each direction. Plant them with a trowel, and dig a hole bigger than the sucker and plant so that the soil mark on the stem sits at the same level as the surface of the soil. It is very important to keep them well watered as they will soon wilt if you have removed them from the parent plant.

Cultivation
These plants do not do well in drought, especially in the first year, and the thing to remember is that they need a lot of water when the flower buds are forming. Keep them well mulched with manure, and straw in the winter to keep off the frost. Feed with general-purpose fertilizer once a month in the summer. When the plants start to develop flower heads in the second and third years, remove the side buds so that only the central one develops on each stem. Take young plants attached to the parent in early spring and, using a knife, sever them from the parent. You can give the young plants away to friends. Replace plants every four years for a really good crop.

Harvesting
Remove the artichokes with secateurs before they start to open; if left any longer, they will be very tough. They open very quickly so check them regularly – you don't want to miss the wonderful feast they will give you. You can keep them in a jug of water with the stalk attached in the fridge if you don't want to eat them straight away. The tender leaf scale bases and the hearts at the bottom are the pieces to eat, but beware of the 'choke' and leathery parts of the leaves – these are inedible! Artichokes are a perfect supper for people who don't know each other very well – they make a good talking point!

Common problems
The main problem with artichokes is slugs and blackfly.

Jerusalem artichoke: Helianthus tuberosus

Life cycle: Perennial.
Site and soil: Not fussy – but does much better in sun with well-drained soil.
Plant: Plant tubers in November when they are fresh, or in February or March.

Unlike the globe artichoke, the Jerusalem artichoke is grown for its edible roots.

Planting distance: For a screen or windbreak plant 30cm (1ft) apart in rows two or three deep; allow 90cm (3ft) between the rows.
Time before harvesting: Eleven months.
How many? Ten to twelve tubers per plant.

Jerusalem artichokes are very underrated as a vegetable. They are lovely and earthy to eat; you can roast them, bake them, fry or stew them, and of course they make great soup. They also have another name – fartichoke; the reason for this is that the carbohydrates are not broken down by the intestines and consequently this causes wind. Maybe this is why we do not take the plant seriously. For the allotment-holder, it is a good plant for many reasons; it breaks up the soil, it will grow where other plants won't, e.g. next to hedges and under trees, as it is able to tolerate shade. It also looks really good grown as a windbreak – it grows up to 3m (10ft) tall and so is ideal for this purpose.

Varieties

'Fusea' is a good one as it is not so knobbly, which makes it much easier to peel than some of the others. 'Boston red' has an attractive rosy skin, but is more difficult to prepare as it is very knobbly. However, as far as taste goes they are all good.

Site and soil

This plant will grow almost anywhere, but is best in full sun and well-drained soil. To give your plants a good start, dig in plenty of well-rotted manure before planting. These plants do cast a lot of shade and because of this you need to think carefully about where they are planted in relation to other vegetables and flowers.

Sowing and planting

You can buy tubers from the greengrocer or from seed catalogues and specialist growers. Plant the tubers with a trowel so that they are about 15cm (6in) deep and 30cm (1ft) apart. Allow 1.25m (4ft) in between rows. If you want to make a screen, plant 30cm (1ft) apart in rows two to three deep and allow 90cm (4ft) between rows. They can be planted in spring but if you plant the shop-bought tubers in November they are much fresher and healthier.

Cultivation

When the stems are about 30cm (1ft) tall, draw up some earth around the roots; this will make the plant more stable. They only need watering in times of real drought and so are very easy to look after as they need little attention. If the site is very windy, the plants may need staking. When the stems are hit by the first frosts, cut them back to 15cm (6in) above the soil.

Harvesting

You can dig up the tubers when needed from late summer right through to autumn and winter. Save a few good tubers and store them in a cool, dark, dry place ready to plant out later. If you want to remove the plants make sure you dig them all up carefully as they will re-grow very readily.

Kale 'Nero di Tosca' is a handsome plant with very dark strap-like leaves.

Common problems
Slugs are a problem as they will damage the tubers. Treat the area with your usual slug deterrent.

Kale: *Brassica oleracea*

Site and soil: An open site with any good well-fed soil.
Sow: Kale can be sowed directly or in modules, in spring or summer.
Harvest: From November to May.
Time before harvesting: Twelve weeks.
How many? Ten per 3m (10ft) row.

Kale is both handsome and tough, and its fresh leaves and shoots can be harvested even in severe winters. There are some gorgeous-looking cultivars available and the black and red ones look fantastic amongst the flower beds.

Varieties
'Nero di Tosca' is a beauty with very dark strap-like leaves and 'Ragged Jack' is an old heritage cultivar, together with 'Redbor' which is curly and dark purple. 'Red Russian' can be eaten raw in salads.

Site and soil
Kale grows best in an open site that has been manured for a previous crop, dug over in the autumn and fertilized with some general purpose food two weeks before planting. Make sure the ground is firm as kale can grow very tall; there is a walking stick kale which can grow to about 90cm (3ft).

Sowing and planting
Sow in modules, around April to June time, transplanting the seedlings six to eight weeks after sowing. It depends on their eventual height as to how much space they need. Usually 60cm (2ft) apart is about right and the rows should be 45cm (18in) apart.

Cultivation
Giving kale plants too much water will make them produce lush growth, which will not see them through the winter months. Keep them well weeded and if they start to look yellow give them a nitrogen feed to perk them up. Scatter some general purpose fertilizer around them in March or April to give them a boost.

Harvesting
Kale can be harvested on a cut-and-come-again basis and this will encourage more growth. When the plants go to seed, stop harvesting as they will then become bitter.

Common problems
The main problems are the same as for cabbage, although clubroot tends not to bother kale as much. Watch out for whitefly.

Leeks: *Allium porrum*

Leeks are an easy and rewarding crop to grow.

Life cycle: Hardy biennial, grown as an annual.
Site and soil: Best on moist, light, heavily-manured soil.
Sow: March and April outdoors.
Time before harvesting: Thirty to forty-five weeks.
How many? Ten to twelve plants per 3m (10ft) row.

Leeks are such fine vegetables – useful, tasty, versatile and easy to grow. You can use the green tops to flavour soups and stews, while the white elongated bulb is great eaten as a vegetable accompaniment or for making soup with potatoes. I find them very reliable and, although they are in the ground for a long time, they can also be harvested over a long period.

Varieties

'Pancho' is a good variety to grow as it is rust-resistant and is an early cropper. 'Apollo' is another recommended variety that has high yields from December onwards. 'Jolant' crops from late summer to late autumn, but will crop later if sown late.

Site and soil

Leeks are best grown on a rich soil that is neutral to slightly acid, and preferably a light sandy loam. Add plenty of organic matter before planting. Choosing the site for sowing leeks may be influenced by the fact that they are left in the soil for a long time and can be there for a year or more. Crop rotation is important for leeks.

Sowing and planting

Leeks are best sown in the greenhouse in modules in midwinter (although they can be sown directly outdoors during March and April), under cover at a temperature of 10°C (50°F). Then when they are pencil-thick and have been hardened off (acclimatized to the weather conditions), plant them out in mid-spring into their final position, using a dibber to make a deep planting hole. It is very satisfying to drop the plant into the hole that you have made and then fill the hole with water.

It is also a good idea to trim the young leeks before transplanting them by taking off a third of the leaves and half of the roots. The soil will fall in by itself and this will help to blanch the stem making the 'nice' bit longer. They should be planted 15cm (6in) deep and 10cm (4in) apart. Allow 30cm (1ft) between rows.

Cultivation

Give your leeks a really good watering in dry spells and hoe between rows when weeds first appear. If time allows, give them a liquid feed during the summer and you will be rewarded with fatter stems; to get them even fatter still, feed them once a week. Leeks benefit from being earthed up (having the soil drawn up around their stems); this will give you a generous amount of white flesh to eat.

Harvesting

You don't need to store your leeks, as they will stay in the ground until the following spring with no problem. You can lift them as you need them, or if you need the ground for another vegetable, just take them up and heel them in somewhere out of the way, laying the leeks in a 'V' shaped trench at a 45° angle until needed.

Common problems

Leeks suffer from rust – orange pustules that can occur especially during damp weather. Try to use a disease-resistant variety.

Lettuce: Lactuca sativa

Life cycle: Half-hardy annual.
Site and soil: Open sunny sites are best, but partial shade is tolerated by midsummer crops.
Time before harvesting: Eleven weeks is the average.
How many? Three lettuces per 1m (3ft) row.

Lettuces are such glorious plants to look at as well as to eat, and there are so many lovely varieties to choose from. They are good to use as edging plants, as a kind of mini edible hedge. Planting alternate red and green varieties makes a very attractive border. The slugs seems to not like the red ones so much and consequently they can provide a little bit of a barrier between the lettuces and other vegetables.

There are basically two types of lettuce – those that form hearts or heads and those that do not. Butterheads, crinkled crispheads and cos types, as well as iceberg, all form very dense heads and are all heart-forming kinds. Mini-lettuces have small hearts. The non-hearting kinds are the cut-and-come-again varieties such as 'Salad Bowl'. The amazing thing about lettuces is that you should be able to harvest them for most of the year if you plan well. By using a cold frame, greenhouse or cloche, and even fleece, you can extend the season by several weeks. They can also be sown in containers and boxes that can be moved according to the weather conditions and look stunning too!

Varieties

Among the mini-lettuces, 'Little Gem' is a cos-type that not only has good texture and flavour but is fast-growing as well as root aphid-resistant. 'Minigreen' is a mini-crisphead type and 'Tom Thumb' is a mini-butterhead with a sweet flavour that is also very hardy, making it ideal for early crops.

Good butterhead varieties include 'Fortune', which is ideal for difficult sites, and 'Valdor', which is an overwintering variety. 'Sangria' has pink-tipped leaves and is resistant to bolting so is well worth considering.

Cos varieties include 'Corsair', which is a medium-sized fast-growing type, and 'Lobjoit's Green', which is a large cos variety with an open head and quite smooth mid-green leaves that are crisp and tasty.

Recommended crisphead varieties are 'Lakeland' and 'Saladin', while 'Beatrice' is an iceberg-type with resistance to root aphids.

Leafy kinds include 'Lollo Rossa', which has an excellent red colour, and both 'Green' and 'Red Salad Bowl' are good because of their reliability as repeat croppers.

Other varieties of salad leaf

Cut-and-come-again salad leaves are a must for the allotment-holder. They are very expensive to buy in the shops and have often been doused with chemicals, so growing your own will not only save you money but will also enable you to have leaves for salads all year round without the chemicals. They are tasty, easy to grow and prolific as well as gorgeous to look at.

Continental and loose-leaf lettuces need the right season to grow well; there are some that are happy growing when it is cold and dark and others that need sun to produce delicious leaves to make your salad. The secret is to select a variety of colours and textures to fill your salad bowl. You can sow them directly into the ground from April to early September or under cloches or make a mini polytunnel a month or six weeks either before or after these dates. Again, this is where the guttering method (see page 73) comes in handy as you can let them grow in the greenhouse then put them out-

Chard is a welcome sight in the dark days of winter.

side when the weather is mild. I divide the soil up in my greenhouse into four sections and sow different leaves in each section as late as November – they take a while to take off but by early March there will be leaves to pick.

Chard is a cut-and-come-again leaf and the 'Rainbow' or 'Bright Lights' varieties make a beautiful addition to both the salad bowl and the winter garden. You can eat the young leaves raw or cook the older leaves as you would spinach. They are best grown from seed in module trays (they take a while to germinate) but you can sow them two or three times a year. You can harvest them about ten to twelve weeks from sowing but you may want to leave a few plants in over the winter just to look at!

Mibuna is a lovely peppery oriental salad leaf, which can be sown every couple of months between March and September. It takes about six weeks to reach maturity. The young leaves can be

Lettuce is a quick, attractive and money-saving crop to grow.

picked when they are a few centimetres high. Mizuna is another very hardy annual oriental cut-and-come-again salad leaf. If you want either Mibuna or Mizuna for salads plant them 10cm (4in) apart; for bigger leaves, plant them 23cm (9in) apart. You should be able to get about four lots of pickings from both of these and other cut-and-come-again varieties.

Other things to try include pak choi, which is very easy and quick to grow and again can be harvested about six weeks after sowing. 'Giant Red Mustard' is a very fast growing salad leaf and in cool weather the red colouring is heightened. Try 'Red Russian' kale for its lovely silver green leaves, and wild rocket which is better grown in cooler conditions as it is much slower to bolt than when grown in the summer.

Try sowing some salad leaves in the spring for late spring or summer picking. Good ones to try are red orach (*Atriplex hortensis var. rubra*), which is wonderful in salads, but can be used in flower arranging as well. It looks particularly attractive amongst the cut flowers. It can reach 1.5m (6ft) tall and produces lovely seed heads. Make sure you use it young for salads. Summer purslane is another good one for an open sunny spot and you can sow this a couple of times during later spring and summer. It is used in Greece for salads and so will cope with a lot of heat. If you keep picking it, it will keep going for up to four months.

Finally lambs lettuce (also known as corn salad) and cress will keep you in leaves for picking during autumn and spring. The first sowings are made in late summer to autumn and the second sowing in late winter to pick in the spring. The August and September sowings will keep you going for several months but the spring sowing will possibly only produce a couple of cuts. These plants will slow down over the winter but as soon as the weather gets warmer they will reward you with some good leaves for salad. They will also give you a reason to go to the allotment and harvest them and tend to them in the colder months.

Site and soil
Lettuces are best grown on moisture-retentive soils that are reasonably fertile, and in full sun so they can grow quickly; if not, they will develop a bitter taste. Mid-summer crops can tolerate light shade.

Sowing and planting
Although many books advise that lettuces should be sown in situ (directly into the ground), I always sow mine in module trays to give them a good start. Sowing directly often results in disappointment as the young plants end up being dug up by animals or birds; there is also a psychological benefit to seeing the lettuces before planting them. The good thing about sowing them in modules is that you can take them out of the modules without disturbing the soil and consequently they will not object. If they are watered in well in their final positions, and you have scattered a couples of handfuls of a general fertilizer over each square metre (yard) two weeks beforehand, they should flourish. Try to sow one seed in each module and plant them out as soon as they are big enough to be handled or before they have six leaves. The base of the leaves should be just above the soil level. If they are planted too deeply they will rot or if not planted deeply enough they will not produce a good shaped lettuce.

I always end up giving loads of lettuces away as it is so easy to sow too many – most people seem to be happy with a lettuce as a present, however. Allow 30cm (1ft) between rows and allow 20cm (8in) for cos varieties, 15cm (6in) for 'Salad Bowl' and 25cm (10in) for butterhead and crisphead types. Start sowing hardy varieties in late February to early March under cloches or in a greenhouse. You can continue sowing until October as long as you check the variety is suitable for the time of year.

Cultivation
It is especially important to water the plants before the hearts reach maturity, as in a dry spell bolting (running to seed) can occur. Keep the area well weeded. Feed winter lettuce in March with a gen-eral fertilizer that can be hoed in along the row. You can also give them a nitrogen-rich fertilizer if they are slow to grow.

Harvesting
Pull or cut the lettuces when you think they look ready for use. You can cut the leafy types leaving just 2.5cm (1in) in the ground to re-grow for a later harvest. If you leave them for too long, however, they will go to seed and become very bitter. Remove the lower leaves and stalks and compost them. Butterheads and non-hearting types go to seed much more quickly than crispheads or cos lettuces.

Common problems
Slugs, snails, cutworms and aphids, as well as birds and rabbits, can all attack your lettuces, so it is best to give them some form of protection. Botrytis and mildew are the worst diseases that occur in wet weather but there are resistant cultivars available.

Onions: *Allium cepa*

Life cycle: Biennial grown as an annual.
Site and soil: A sunny spot is essential. The soil should be limed if it is too acidic.
Sow: March or April for maincrop varieties for storing; mid August for Japanese varieties for early summer harvesting; mid-August for selected varieties for earlier ripening than main crop sowing; March to August for spring onions.
Time before harvesting: twenty-five weeks (spring-sown); forty-five weeks (overwintered).
How many? Spring onions – sixty per 1m (3ft) row; onions – seven per 1 m (3ft) row.

Onions are a must for nearly all types of cuisine – food from all around the world is dependent on onions to give a good flavour. Onions are easy to grow and have a long storage life. They are a fantastic crop to harvest and then there is the joy of stringing them and seeing them hanging up in the shed. The introduction of heat-treated onions sets now means that growing onions is easy even for the beginner.

Varieties
Onion sets are immature onions – small, part-

Onions should be dried before storing.

grown onion bulbs. Heat-treated sets include 'Hyduro', which are large, and have golden-brown skin, and 'Red Barron', which have a shiny, dark crimson skin. Recommended untreated sets include 'Centurion', which is a great strong-growing onion that gives a heavy early maturing crop that stores well. 'Sturgeon' is also very popular, easy to come by and stores well over winter. For onion seed, 'Buffalo' is a hybrid that can be sown in autumn or spring. For overwintering, 'Senshy' and 'Sonic' are both good choices.

Site and soil

Onions prefer a sunny position with a rich but light soil. However, they will do well in most soil as long as it is firm. For this reason it is best to prepare the soil well in advance of planting. Dig the soil to 45cm (18in) deep and work in organic matter. Just before planting, tread down the soil so that it is firm.

Sowing and planting

If you want a supply of onions all year round, sow seed or plant sets twice in a year, first in midwinter to mid-spring, and then again in the autumn. The overwintered crops are more susceptible to disease but treated seeds are available to protect against fungal disease. Never sow in a cold spell.

Onion sets are easier to handle and more con-

venient as they have already started into growth. 225g (½lb) of sets will be enough to plant a 10.5 m (35ft) row. Use a trowel to plant them and just leave the tips visible above the soil, making sure you pull off the wispy tail – if not, the birds will come and dig them up. Space the sets 19cm (4in) apart. After planting, check your sets from time to time to make sure they have not been dislodged by birds or worms. Sets tend to do better in colder areas and are less likely to be plagued by onion fly.

If you are sowing seed, try to avoid transplanting them as onions tend to run to seed quickly if their growth pattern is interrupted. Sow them in drills 1cm (½in) deep and 30cm (1ft) apart in rows. Spring onions and pickling onions can be sown much closer. Onions should be treated differently according to their type. Maincrop onion seed and sets should be sown outside from mid-March. If they are sown under cloche protection, they can be sown four weeks earlier. Japanese onion seed should be sown outside in mid-August. Spring or salad onions should be sown at three-week intervals from early April to early June.

Cultivation

Using an onion hoe, regularly weed your plants as they do not have the above-ground growth to suppress weeds. Make sure you keep them well watered between April and June and cut the flower heads off as soon as they appear as these will not store well.

Cultivation of shallots is exactly the same as for onions. Plant at the end of winter or beginning of spring. When the foliage starts to turn yellow in mid-summer, do not apply any more water as this is the time to let the bulbs dry off. Check regularly for signs of disease. If the weather is very wet, cover them with cloches.

Harvesting

Maincrop onions can be harvested from August onwards; Japanese varieties from late June; late July for selected autumn-sown varieties; May to March for spring onions; August for pickling onions; and June or July onwards for overwintering sets.

A good way of drying onions is to use four stout posts with chicken wire stretched across them. You can also them knot them together and hang them up in the shed until you need them. However, remember that autumn-sown and autumn-planted onions do not store well, so they should be used as soon as they are ready.

Common problems

Eelworm and onion fly are the two main pests for the onion crop, while mildew, white rot and neck rot are the most common diseases. White rot is a common and serious fungal disease. It can survive in the soil for many years and can move through the soil to infect new plants, so it is important to dig up and burn any infected plants. Onion fly larvae feed on the stems and bulbs. Flies are attracted to newly disturbed earth, so it is best to sow onion seeds in a stale seed bed, i.e. one you have prepared about ten days earlier, and cover the seed bed with fine netting. You can grow onions in the same soil for several years but as soon as you see signs of pests or diseases make sure you move them and practise crop rotation.

Parsnips: *Pastinaca sativa*

Life cycle: Hardy biennial grown as an annual.
Site and soil: The best soil is rich and slightly heavy.
Sow: February to May.
Time before harvesting: Six to eleven months.

How many? About fourteen medium-sized parsnips per 3m (10ft) row.

Parsnips are the epitome of long winter days, sitting by the fire and eating roast dinners around the table with family and friends. Parsnips improve in quality as the winter progresses and are especially good if a frost gets to the roots. Parsnips can be boiled, baked or fried, and their leaves can be eaten as a green vegetable. They are very hardy plants. It is wise to leave a few roots to go to seed as they have beautiful flowers that attract 'good' insects such as hoverflies.

Varieties

'Tender and True' is a long-rooted, canker-resistant variety, whilst 'Gladiator' is a good variety to grow on a light sandy soil. 'Gladiator' is early to mature and is canker-resistant.

Site and soil

Soil is the most important thing to consider when growing parsnips. If you have a thin soil that is very gravelly, you will only get small forked roots. The best soils are rich and slightly on the heavy side. The ideal pH is 6.5. Manure the soil in the previous season. Parsnips have a low nitrogen requirement.

Seed sowing

Sow directly as parsnips, because of their tap root, do not like transplanting. However, they can be successfully started off in deep module trays then very carefully transplanted, ensuring that their roots are not disturbed and taking out the whole plug and planting it.

Germination is slow and if you are sowing directly into the ground, sow two or three seeds per station with a couple of radish seeds. The radishes will be mature by the time the parsnips come up and they will help you to see where the parsnips are.

Cultivation

When the seedlings germinate, thin them out to leave the strongest ones and make sure to keep them weed-free. Keep them well spaced out to get good strong plants and only water when there has been no rain as they are good at resisting drought.

Parsnips can be left in the soil until required.

Harvesting

You can start to lift your parsnips in late summer when they will be 'baby' vegetables. I like to wait until after the first frosts when the starch in the parsnips has turned to sugar and they are at their sweetest. They can be left in the ground but also stored in clamps.

Common problems

Apart from the carrot fly, parsnip canker can be a major problem so try to buy resistant cultivars.

Peas: Pisum sativum

Life cycle: Half-hardy annual.
Site and soil: Sun or partial shade, protected from strong wind. The soil needs to be moisture-retentive. There is no need to add nitrogen.
Sow: Late February to mid-March under cloches; late March to mid-June in the open; late June to mid-July in the open for autumn crop; October to November under cloches for spring harvesting.
Time before harvesting; First earlies – twelve weeks; second earlies – fourteen weeks; maincrop varieties – fifteen weeks.
How many? 3kg (6lb to 7lb) per 1m (3ft) row.

To have fresh peas is a wonderful treat; in fact, all too often they don't even get as far as the table as every time you walk past them it is just too tempting to pick some and eat them there and then. Peas are a good example of the difference between shop-bought vegetables and those that are freshly picked. It is possible to have peas for many weeks, and sitting on a sunny doorstep to shell them is a job that always reminds me of my childhood.

Varieties

Among the earlies, 'Kelvedon Wonder' is a vigorous and reliable cropper and has received the award of garden merit. 'Hurst Green Shaft' has a great taste and good disease-resistance and grows to 75cm (2.5ft); this is a second early. A good maincrop variety is 'Onward', which is very prolific. A mangetout variety that is delicious is 'Delikett'; its pods are picked and cooked whole before the peas fatten. Sugar snap peas grow to 2m (6ft) and are also eaten whole; they produce fat pods, as opposed to mangetout pods which are flat.

Site and soil

Peas like lots of sun, although in the middle of summer they can tolerate a bit of shade. They are nitrogen-fixing, like other legumes, and as usual for this group of plants they are very greedy. They do not tolerate drought and need the usual good start with plenty of organic matter or garden compost.

Sowing

Geoff Hamilton's technique of sowing early peas in guttering was demonstrated on *Gardener's World* and this is just one of his many brilliant ideas. This method will allow you to sow early under cover in March, before putting your peas outside in April when the weather is warm. Choose a hardy variety such as 'Feltham First' and sow the peas into lengths of plastic guttering, leaving them inside to germinate. Push them down into the soil about 2.5cm (1in) deep and 5cm (2in) apart. This method also stops the peas from rotting, as they hate the cold and wet. Place the guttering in a mouse-free area to avoid having your plants nibbled.

You can sow seeds directly into the soil in 'U'-shaped drills with flat bottoms for the second early varieties. To work out the distance between rows,

Peas and mangetout – there is no better taste than a freshly picked pea, but make sure you leave some to take home!

the equivalent of the ultimate height of the crop should be a guide. You can grow catch crops such as lettuces or radishes in between. To maintain a steady supply, sow an early variety every four weeks until midsummer or make a single sowing of an early, second early and maincrop variety, each of which will mature at different times.

Cultivation

Peas do need to be supported; it is useful to keep some of your prunings, as long as they are twiggy, for this job. When the peas are about 8cm (3in) tall, push the branches among your peas to support them. The other way to do it is to surround them with canes and string or chicken wire if you cannot find any twiggy pea sticks. If birds are a problem, lay netting over the peas to protect them.

Harvesting

Pick the peas as late as you can before eating them

to maximize the sweetness, and try to pick them two or three times a week so they can form more pods. Pinching them out will help the peas to set and make the plant bush out, increasing the yield. You can eat the pea tips in salad.

Common problems

Pea moth can ruin crops, so try to protect your crop with a fine mesh. Birds, mice, thrips and aphids are all pests of peas and powdery mildew is a common disease. Choose resistant cultivars to avoid mildew.

Potatoes: Solanum tuberosum

Life cycle: Half-hardy annual.
Site and soil: Sunny, well-dug and composted. Do not add lime.
Planting: Mid- to late March for early varieties; April for second early and main crop varieties.
Time before harvesting: Potatoes are grouped according to their season of lifting. Earlies mature in around 110 days from planting to harvest, second earlies in 110 to120 days, and maincrops in 125 to 140 days.
How many? Earlies: 1kg (2.2lb) per 3m (10ft) row 75cm (2ft6in) wide. Slightly fewer for maincrop.

Until the 1800s potatoes were only grown by the poor. However, over the past 200 years the potato's nutritional value and taste have been appreciated more and it is now part of the staple diet of many countries. First discovered in the Andes Mountains in South America in 1537, the potato is a vegetable really worth growing. It is an excellent weed sup-presser due to its canopy of leaves and is great for breaking up the soil, so consequently is a good first crop for your allotment.

Digging up potatoes is a wonderful job; I always marvel at the warmth of the soil when you put your hand in to take out the potatoes. If you need to make a choice about which ones to plant then go for earlies, as these are the ones that provide new potatoes. They also take up less room, are less like-ly to get diseases and will be available for harvest when shop-bought ones are more expensive.

Earthing up potatoes will encourage more tubers to form.

Varieties

'Arran Pilot' is an early potato. It is an old variety and produces a heavy crop of white potatoes. 'Red Duke of York' has pale yellow flesh and is rich, and sweet and good for baking. For a second early, choose 'Charlotte'; this has a firm yellow flesh and a good flavour, and is good both for salads and for boiling. 'Kondor' is a red-skinned variety that has a firm flesh, making it good for roasting and baking. Maincrop types include the waxy potato 'Desiree', which is a good all-rounder. 'Nicola' is worth considering as it is resistant to eelworm and blight and is a good boiling variety.

Site and soil

Potatoes will really grow on almost any soil, but if you want good yields then fairly rich ground that has been dug and manured in the autumn and winter previous to planting is best. Try to avoid frost pockets – don't forget that potatoes are not frost-resistant. Make sure you have some horticultural fleece or newspaper to throw over your early varieties if a frost is threatened, especially if they have produced leaves and stems at this time. First-time gardeners are often advised to grow potatoes to clean up the ground, but it is the earthing up and cultivation of the soil that does this – not the potato tuber itself!

Planting

Potatoes sold for planting are known as seed potatoes. It is important to buy these rather than rake some out of the bottom of the larder as they will not be certified virus-free. This is very important as potatoes are prone to so many pests and diseases. You can buy them in February from a garden centre or by mail order (there is a huge variety to choose from). You will find that a 3 kg (7lb) bag will plant up a 9m (10yd) row of earlies, or a 14m (15yd) row of second earlies or maincrop potatoes. When you receive your seed potatoes, sit them in egg boxes or seed trays so that the end with the most buds or 'eyes' points topmost. Then put your potatoes in a place that receives light but is frost-free. The buds or 'eyes' will then start to grow and when they are about 2.5cm (1in) long they will be ready to plant. The process is known as chitting and you should get a better, earlier crop from your potatoes if you 'chit' them before planting.

Don't bother to chit second earlies or main crop potatoes. Some people say you should remove all but three of the shoots on each potato, or cut potatoes in half to save money – I don't do either of these things as it is more likely that the potatoes will become infected with viruses from a dirty knife if cut in half; in any case, seed potatoes are not that expensive.

Try to aim to plant them out around St Patrick's Day (17 March). It always helps to remember dates to plant out things if they are associated with a particular day! There are two methods of planting; you can either dig a trench or plant them in individual holes using a trowel. Be careful how you handle the potatoes as you can easily knock off the shoots. Plant them 15cm (6in) deep. Space them 30cm (12in) apart with 60cm (2ft) between rows for earlies, and 40–75cm (16–30in) for maincrops. Planting them too close together will give you smaller potatoes at harvest time. After you have planted them, rake in a little general fertilizer, about two handfuls to each 1m (3ft) part of the row.

Cultivation

Earth up the shoots (the leaves and stems of potatoes are called the haulms) as soon as they appear. This is to protect them from the frost so make sure you do this if it is cold. Otherwise you can wait until they are 15cm (6in) high and then use a hoe to pull the earth up so that only the tips are showing. This also helps with keeping the tubers from turning green, making them inedible. Make sure the potatoes do not dry out in the spring so water them well if necessary at that time.

Harvesting

Harvesting your potatoes is such a pleasure. If you have children, try to involve them in this – their faces are usually a picture when digging up these warm jewels of the allotment. When the potatoes are in flower they are usually ready for lifting. Use a fork and be careful not to stab your potatoes, as this will damage them. Earlies are not suitable for storing and need to be eaten straight away but maincrop potatoes can be stored in paper sacks available from your seed potato stockist. Dry them off for a few hours on the soil surface before storing. Keep them in the dark to avoid sprouting.

Common problems

Between 1846 and 1851 over a million people died in Ireland due to the potato blight. This is an indication that crop rotation is really important for this vegetable. Potato blight is more likely in wet seasons. Always start with new certified seed potatoes and ensure no tubers are left in the ground after harvesting. Cut off any foliage immediately if it shows signs of the blight (dark brown or black blotches on leaves, sometimes fringed with white fungus).

Wire worms are the larvae of click beetles, and these feed on the tubers. They tend to be more prevalent on newly cultivated ground and you will see evidence of tunneling in the tubers. Scab can be a problem – it is more likely on alkaline soils, but does not really affect the taste. Buy resistant varieties.

Pumpkin and winter squash: Cucurbita maxima, C. moschata and C. pepo

Life cycle: Annual.
Site and soil: An open sunny site is essential with fertile, well-drained soil.
Sow: April indoors; May in the open.
Plant: Late May to early June.
Time before harvesting: Five months.
How many? This will depend on the variety, but generally there will be either one large fruit or four to six small fruits per plant.

Pumpkins and winter squashes are a diverse group in terms of shape, colour and size; they are really quite extraordinary. They are really fast growers, and great for the allotment as they attract children

Pumpkin and squash are easy to grow, and are great for encouraging children to have a go at gardening.

to have a go at gardening as well as providing an autumnal treat for adults. They really love rich soil and can be easily grown on the compost heap where they will have a direct line to nutrients. However, the really big pumpkins will need to be grown on the ground. They are fantastic for Hallowe'en carving, and for use in soups. You can also eat the seeds of some types, plus the flowers, tendrils and shoot tips. They also look really beautiful displayed in a bowl or on the table. They do, however, need a long hot growing season.

Varieties

Among the pumpkins, 'Atlantic Giant' is a trailing exhibition type, and has huge fruits if you want to grow record-breaking fruit. 'Baby Bear' is a trailing, miniature type that has orange fruits that are good for storing. 'Ghost Rider' is, as its name suggests, a Hallowe'en type with edible seeds. For winter squash, choose 'Crown Prince' with its blue skin and orange flesh and sweet nutty flavour. This stores well over winter if you keep it cool and dry. 'Cobnut' is one of the earliest maturing butternut pumpkins and is suitable for cooler climates as it has a longer ripening time. This is great for roasting. The variety 'Sweet Dumpling' is also recommended because you can grow it over an arch very successfully and it looks fantastic during late summer and early autumn.

Site and soil

The most important thing for pumpkins and squashes is a good rich soil, so add bucketfuls of manure or garden compost before planting. This is best done in the spring time when you can dig a large hole and fill it with compost or manure. Make sure you have plenty of room for the pumpkins to grow as they need a lot of space. They can cope with dappled shade, as long as they have rich soil to keep them happy.

Seed sowing

It is best to start squash and pumpkins off under glass as they need a temperature of 13°C (56°F) to germinate. Sow two or three seeds to a small pot, and when the young plants are about 8cm (3in) high, thin them to one seedling, the strongest one. You can use the airing cupboard for this if you don't have a heated propagator. Make sure you label them really well as it is very easy to confuse pumpkins, marrows, courgettes, squashes and cucumbers with each other. It makes sense to colour code the different types of the *Cucurbita* family as they can get confusing.

Planting

Plant out in late spring or early summer, ideally in warm soil; you can warm the soil by putting cloches or fleece over it. It is wise to put a bell cloche over your pumpkins so that the slugs don't eat them when they are young. You will need to plant bush types 90cm (3ft) apart, and the trailing cultivars 1.5m (5ft) apart. The rows will need to be the same distance apart as the spacing.

Cultivation

Never let the plants go short of water and make sure you feed them once a week, and of course make sure they are kept weed-free. If you have small varieties such as 'Sweet Dumpling', you can erect an arch to grow them over. Try to get hold of some sweet chestnut or hazel poles and attach a piece of wood across the top to form an arch. For the larger types, pinch the shoot tip out when eight leaves have formed and make sure that the long shoots are kept in check so they do not roam too far. Remove all but four of the fruits, or all but one if you want to grow a whopper. I always use a tile to stand my pumpkins on when they are developing; this stops them from getting wet and rotting as they sometimes do if you leave them lying on the soil.

Harvesting

It is best to wait until the first frosts have killed off the leaves before harvesting the fruits. They should have a good colour and a hollow ring when tapped. Leave them in the sun to allow their skins to harden. If you intend to store them, use the larger more mature types. They will keep for months, sometimes until spring time if you are lucky.

Common problems

Powdery mildew or cucumber mosaic virus are the only real threat to the crops so make sure the plants have plenty of air around them. Slugs and snails are likely to attack the seedlings, so protect them with cloches.

Radish: Raphanus sativus

Life cycle: Hardy annual or biennial.
Site and soil: Most soils dug well.
Sow: February under cloches; March to August in the open and July and August winter radish outside.
Harvest: April to September, or October to March for winter radish varieties.
Time before harvesting: Summer varieties, three to eight weeks; winter varieties, three to five months.
How many? Summer varieties: 0.5 kg (1lb) per 1m (3ft) row. Winter varieties: 1kg (2.2lb) per 1m (3ft) row.

Radishes are so fast growing and, like children, seem to grow before your eyes. Consequently they are a good choice for the children's plot, if you have one on your allotment. The word 'radish' is derived from the Saxon for rude (of course, young children will love that) *rudo*, or *read* (ruddy), or from the Sanskrit *rudhira*, meaning blood, referring to the bright red colour of the vegetables. Originally from China, they reached Mediterranean areas even before ancient Greek times. They are a staple food in Japan and China.

Varieties

'Cherry Belle' is a variety with round, scarlet red roots and 'French Breakfast' is an elongated radish with a crisp, mild flavour. For winter radish, choose between 'Black Spanish', which has black flesh, and is an old variety that is very suitable for cold areas, or 'Minowase Summer Cross', which is a white-skinned, long, Japanese-type with a delicate flavour.

Site and soil

Radishes like the sun, but at the same time prefer cool conditions; if they are grown in conditions that are too hot, they will run to seed (bolt) very quickly. They are a very good companion plant, especially when grown with parsnips, as they are quick to germinate, unlike parsnips, allowing you to see where your parsnips will come up. In spring and late autumn, when radishes need the sun most, they make a good intercropping plant for peas and beans as these legumes will be short or cut down at this time; then in the hotter summer months the legumes will shade the radishes, which will be very welcome. Their needs are simple, just a well-dug soil to the depth of 15cm (6in), with no stones or fresh compost in it.

Sowing and planting

Sow small amounts of radish seed frequently to make sure you have a constant supply rather than a glut. For your summer varieties, begin sowing in mid-April and continue at three-week intervals to mid-September. For winter varieties, sow at the end of July at three-week intervals until mid-September. The drills should be 1cm (½in) deep. Radishes fail to develop properly unless they are thinned quickly. Thin ordinary varieties to 2.5cm (1in) and winter types to 15cm (6in). If you want to grow more than one row, make sure they are 30cm (1ft) apart; or for summer radishes, 15cm (6in) apart.

Cultivation

Make sure that the plants are kept well watered or they will become woody and inedible. The best way to grow them is to make sure they develop quickly, so hoe between rows to avoid competition from weeds.

Harvesting

Pull the summer types as soon as they are an edible size. You can leave the winter radishes in the soil until they are needed, or you can lift them in late autumn and store the roots in boxes of sand, cutting off their tops first. They are delicious grated and eaten raw in salads. You can also eat the tops.

Common problems

Flea beetles are attracted to radishes but plants are not usually made inedible by them. If you keep the plants well watered and weeded they will still grow on strongly. You could also grow them under horticultural fleece.

Rhubarb: Rheum x cultorum

Life cycle: Perennial.
Site and soil: Sunny spot; with well-drained moisture-retentive soil. Rhubarb does not like to be waterlogged in the winter.
Plant: March.
Planting distance: 90cm (3ft) apart, and space the rows 30cm (12in) apart.
Time before harvesting: Wait for one year before harvesting as this will allow the plants to build up energy.
How many? Take one third to half of the stems at a time.

Rhubarb is such a delightful plant. It looks fantastic when its stems are just showing through and, interplanted with bulbs such as beetroot-coloured hyacinths, it makes a wonderful spring display. It is classed as a vegetable and unfortunately is often overlooked to make way for other things. Try to make space for it – it will provide you with structure and also give you luscious stems to eat for many months.

Varieties

'Champagne' is an early variety with long bright scarlet stems and a good flavour. 'Cawood Castle' is a very vigorous variety and very tasty. 'Timperley Early' has received the Royal Horticultural Society Award of Garden Merit as it is a reliable plant, with excellent flavour, and crops well.

Site and soil

Before making your rhubarb bed, make sure it is sited in a sunny position with well-drained fertile soil that is moisture-retentive. I like to grow three varieties that are early, mid- and late season types

Using a rhubarb forcer will give you tender, pink stems to eat early in the year.

so you can harvest it for a long time; so careful preparation of the soil is very important. Dig it over in the autumn and add a very generous amount of manure or garden compost. If the soil is not well drained, the crowns will rot.

Sowing and planting

It is perfectly possible to grow rhubarb from seed, but it takes a long time to establish and I think it is better to buy some plants or acquire some from a friend. Plant the crowns 5cm (2in) below the surface of the soil and 1m (3ft) apart in March. Make sure you firm them in using your boot. It is best not to harvest them in the first year as they need to build up strength.

Cultivation

Your rhubarb will need feeding, especially with nitrogen. I use pelleted chicken manure or garden compost as this helps it to produce green leaves, from which the leaf petioles will produce your crop. Remove any flowers and make sure you keep plants weed-free. If you cover the crown with a rhubarb forcer or bucket stuffed with straw in January, you can harvest some tender pink sticks in March. After being forced the plants will need a rest, so give them a monthly feed from April to July so they can build up their strength again. Try to alternate the crowns that you force each year so they don't run out of energy. Keep them well watered in the first season.

Harvesting

Stems that have not been forced can be harvested until the end of June; after that they start to get tough and green. Hold the stalk at the base, pull down and twist it. Start with the outer sticks and work inwards, but never harvest more than half the stalks.

Common problems

Make sure you get virus-free stock to begin with. As usual slugs and snails are a pest to the young stems. Honey fungus can attack your plants and crown rot could be an issue if you have not provided free-draining soil.

Runner beans: *Paseolus coccineus*

Life cycle: Perennial but grown in the UK as a half-hardy annual.
Site and soil: Full sun, sheltered from wind, in well-dug, water-retaining soil.
Sow: Either indoors or under protection from mid-March to April or outside when any danger of frost has passed in May.
Plant outside: In late May or early June.
Time before harvesting: Thirteen weeks.
How many? 5kg (11lb) per metre (yard).

Runner beans are so worthwhile to grow; not only do they taste good, but they look good as well, and give you lots to eat over a long period of time if you take the trouble to prepare for their arrival. They also provide some structure on the allotment and this can be left in over the winter as well to give

*Runner beans
need a support
to climb up.*

some interest. In their natural habitat, they will grow high up into the mountains, using trees to climb up. However, remember that their foliage is very dense and this means they can cast deep shade over a large area. For this reason it is best the rows run north–south so that the sun can get round both sides of the rows.

Varieties

There is a huge variety of runner beans to choose from. 'Lady Di' is a recent variety bred in the late princess's honour, with lovely bright red flowers. 'White Lady' has received the RHS Award of Garden Merit and has white flowers and high yields late into the season; it also has the advantage of being stringless.

Site and soil

Runner beans prefer a position in full sun, although they will tolerate part-shade very well. Because of their height, they should not be grown in areas exposed to winds as they will easily be blown over.

Do not add nitrogen to the soil as runner beans, being in the legume family, are nitrogen fixing, so if you add nitrogen it will result in the plants producing too much foliage and no flowers, and consequently no beans. The ideal soil should be deeply dug with lots of well-rotted organic matter incorporated; this will help the soil to hold onto the moisture, which is the key to growing a good runner bean crop. It helps to dig out a trench in November the year before, 60cm (2ft) wide and 23cm (9in) deep. You can then put in any organic garden waste, anything that will rot down and also fill it up with newspaper in January, then two weeks before planting put in some fertilizer. This will really help establish your beans.

Seed sowing

If you really love runner beans, then do two sowings – one in April and one in June. This means you will have beans from July until October. If you go away on holiday in the summer, you can time it so they are ready to pick when you return, but don't forget to ask your allotment neighbour to water them while you are away.

Before sowing your seed, you must make sure you have a good support system. I find the best way

and the most secure is to use 2.25m (8ft) canes, or even better, hazel poles, and push them into the soil 60cm (2ft) apart, then tie them together at the top. They need to be 35cm (15in) apart along the row. Use wire rather than twine to tie them together as they are less likely to give when the beans get heavy or in a strong wind.

If you are sowing directly into the ground it is important to wait until all danger of frost has passed and then make sure you sow three seeds at the bottom of each cane; growing three is an insurance policy as they often get eaten by birds, snails and slugs, and you can easily pull out two seedlings if they all grow. The beans should be planted 5cm (2in) deep. It is good to start them off in pots in April in the greenhouse and then plant them out, holding some back if necessary to fill in for any that get eaten by pests.

Cultivation

Tie the shoots to the poles carefully to help them climb (they will not climb unless they are touching something). Sweet pea rings are ideal for this. In just a couple of days they will have started to find their way up the poles. Keep the weeds down by either putting down a membrane when you first erect the canes or you can use straw to put in the middle of the support. Grass clippings also make a good mulch in June.

Flowering time is the most important time to keep them watered. To help with pollination you can plant some sweet peas among them to attract pollinating insects.

When the shoots have reached the top of the canes, pinch them out to prevent them getting top-heavy and give them a really good liquid feed in August – this will give a boost to the end-of-the-season yield.

Harvesting

Pick the beans when they are young as the old ones become very stringy and are not good to eat, but it is useful to save them for sowing next year.

Common problems

Blackfly and drying out at the roots can be a problem.

Spinach: Spiniacia oleracea

Life cycle: Hardy annual.
Site and Soil: Needs a fertile, moisture-retentive soil. Does not like poor or stony soil.
Sow: You can sow it from mid-winter to early autumn every three weeks
Harvest: Sever the whole plant or use as a cut-and-come-again crop.
Time before harvesting: Ten to twelve weeks.

Spinach is great eaten raw in salads or equally delicious if lightly steamed. Spinach also makes a good catch crop (grown while waiting for a long-term crop to be planted). It is a cold-tolerant plant and so suffers in the summer (if you want an all year round crop, spinach beet or chard is better). However, nothing beats the taste, so get the conditions right and you will be rewarded with a fantastic crop.

Varieties
'Senic' variety gives a high yield and is resistant to mildew and is also suitable for cut-and-come-again. 'Atlanta' is hardy for winter use and 'Monnopa' with its thick leaves is slow to bolt.

Site and soil
The best soil for spinach will contain plenty of nutrients and be very moisture-retentive. A slightly shady spot in the summer is helpful, and don't think about growing it in soil which has a low fertility or is very dry. If you intercrop it with taller vegetables. they will provide some dappled shade at the hottest time of the day for your spinach. Add pelleted chicken manure if fertility is low.

Sowing and planting
When you cook spinach it seems to shrink a lot, so sow plenty of it. It can be sown directly into the soil about 1cm (½in) deep in rows 30cm (12in) apart. As it does not germinate in very hot conditions, make your first sowings in mid-winter and continue to sow at three-week intervals until early summer. You can start further sowings in the autumn when the weather has cooled down and this will give you a supply of leaves into the winter. If you want to grow large plants you can sow small clumps of seeds about 15cm (6in) apart. If you just want small leaves for salad, make a wide drill and just scatter in the seeds; you won't need to thin them and you can just harvest them when needed for your salad.

Cultivation
Keep your spinach well watered at all times; if not, the plants will bolt and go to seed. Give it a high nitrogen feed if growth slows down. Keep it weeded and mulched to keep moisture in.

Harvesting
Cut off the plant to just above the ground, allowing some stem so it can re-sprout. Alternatively, just pick individual leaves when required.

Common problems
Pigeons can be a problem as well as greenfly. Downy mildew can cause problems but resistant cultivars are available.

Sweet corn: Zea mays

Life cycle: Grown as an annual.
Site and soil: Needs plenty of sun and shelter and good well-drained soil.
Sow: April indoors or in a greenhouse and early May outdoors.
Harvest: August and September.
Time before harvesting: Twelve weeks.
How many? Six to nine cobs per square metre (1 yard).

Make sure you get the water on the boil before picking your corn as the sugars start to turn to starch as soon as they are picked! You only get one or two cobs per plant but they are really worth growing as they can taste superb and most children love them too. They do better in the milder weather, but they are always worth a try. The mouth-watering cobs are also very nutritious, each cob giving roughly twenty-two per cent of the daily requirement for vitamins A and C, Magnesium and Iron.

Varieties
Choose from 'Ovation', which is a mid-season supersweet yellow variety, 'Honey Bantam' (yellow

Sweetcorn should be cooked as soon as it is picked to prevent the sugars turning to starch.

and white with an excellent flavour) or 'Red Strawberry' (a novelty type with berry-shaped small cobs bearing tiny red kernels).

Site and soil

Try using a green manure with the ability to fix nitrogen, such as alfalfa or clover, in the preceding autumn. You can leave the crop in place and dig in a few weeks before planting. Sun and shelter are essential for sweetcorn; if not, they will not flower. They also need moisture; if not, they will not come to much, so make sure that their strong roots have some moist but well-drained soil.

Sowing and planting

I always sow my seeds in individual pots of compost indoors or in a greenhouse in late April and plant them out in May when danger of frost is past.

The corn must be well-pollinated if you want some good cobs and the best way to do this is to plant them in blocks. The spiky male flowers or tassels stand above the female flowers with silks. The female flowers appear in the leaf axils, both on the same plant, and are wind-pollinated. Block planting will ensure good pollination.

Plant them out in late May in the south or early June in the north. Make sure they are properly hardened off (acclimatized to the outside elements) before planting out about 45cm (18in) apart both ways.

Cultivation

You do not need to water these plants until they start to flower, when the soil should be kept moist. If the site is windy, earth up the plants to give them more stability. When the male flowers open at the top of the plant, give them a tap regularly to discharge the pollen onto the female flowers lower down the stem.

Harvesting

When the cobs are ripe, they start to lean further away from the stem and the tassels begin to dry up and turn brown. Some people suggest sticking a fingernail into the cobs to test if they are ready, but this can spoil them.

Common problems

Birds, squirrels and badgers may strip your crop and mice are attracted to the seeds. Poor pollination can be a problem which may lead to gaps in the row of ripe kernels. Crop rotation will help to control attacks from fruit flies.

Tomatoes: Lycopersicon esculentum

Life cycle: Perennial grown as an annual in the UK.
Site and soil: Full sun, well drained, water-retentive soil.
Sow: Mid-March to early April indoors or in a greenhouse.
Plant: Early May under cloches or late May to early June outside when danger of frost has passed.
Harvest: July to September.
Time before harvesting: Fourteen weeks, but this could vary depending on the variety and where they are grown (i.e. in the glasshouse or outdoors).
How many? 2–3 kg (4.5–6.5lb) per tomato plant.

You simply have to grow tomatoes as they are so rewarding; and of course they are so versatile – even the green ones are useful for making chutney. They are also a crop which can be harvested well into autumn and I have even been known to have a couple left on Christmas day! They are fun to grow from seed and another good crop to start children off with.

Your options are indoor or glasshouse tomatoes, usually grown on a single stem (also known as vine or indeterminate), or the outdoor variety of cordon tomatoes. The indoor ones tend to be more tender and prefer the protection of a glasshouse. You can also grow bush tomatoes (also known as determinate), which will not require so much attention. Another alternative is the hanging basket or container types, which make compact growth. There are so many kinds to choose from – beefsteak, cherry, orange, black, stripy, giants, round, flattened, plum or elongated varieties. Spend some time poring over the catalogues until you find the ones that best suit you. It can be fun to experiment with a few new types each year but also stick to the old faithfuls to be sure of a good harvest. Try to write out the labels before you start sowing as it is all to easy to get distracted and then not know which ones are which.

Tomatoes are generally thought to have been brought back from Central America by the Spanish Conquistadors, although another legend suggests that two Jesuit priests brought them to Italy from Mexico. It was thought to have become a good food crop from around AD 400 so it has been around for quite a while. They were known as 'love apples' in *Gerard's Herbal*, and were thought of as an aphrodisiac. However, the Elizabethans thought the red colour represented danger, not helped by the knowledge that they are in the same family as deadly nightshade (*Solonaceae*)!

Many of us seem to have good memories of growing and harvesting tomatoes, either with our parents in the greenhouse picking them or with our own children stuffing as many as possible into their mouths. Whatever they remind you of, their smell and taste is certainly evocative and, served in a salad with basil and mozarella cheese, there is nothing to beat them!

Varieties

Among the bush tomatoes, 'Alfresco' is a heavy cropping plant with a good flavour. 'Tumbler' is a spreading variety and consequently good for hanging baskets. Among the cherry tomatoes, 'Gardener's Delight' can be grown indoors or outside as cordons and has small, sweet fruits. 'Sun Baby' is a yellow, sweet variety, again with small fruits. 'Sweet Million' is worth trying as it is a heavy cropper with thin skins and very small fruits. Among the plum tomatoes, 'Olivade' has won the RHS Award of Garden Merit and has large, dark red fruits that are very early to mature. These can be grown outside or under glass. If you want to grow vine tomatoes, 'Sungold' is a must; it has orange fruits growing on the vine and also has some virus-resistance. 'Tigerella' has striped fruits and a very good flavour. 'Brandywine' is a traditional Amish pink cordon type and it is famous for its enormous fruits and fantastic flavour; the colours vary from yellow to maroon, making it great for salads. Some of the unusual Mediterranean and other less common types tend to have a semi-indeterminate habit; some of the stems end in flowers and others trail all over the place and are very unruly. These ones are very high-maintenance as you will need to keep a constant eye out for their straggly shoots and make sure you preserve the flowers.

Site and soil

There is a lot of advice available on growing tomatoes, but the most important thing to remember is that they need the sunniest part of your allotment to be really successful.

Growing tomatoes well is about preparation. For outdoor cordon types (a cordon is a single stem), mark out an area allowing 38–45cm (15–18in) between each plant and 90cm (36in) in between each single or staggered double row. The area then needs to be dug over about two to three weeks before planting and lots of organic matter should be incorporated in the top 30cm (12in). Cover the area with a good quality membrane and make crosses with a knife where each plant is to go. Each tomato requires a stake and these need to be at least 1.5m (4ft 6in) high; you could use a piece of one-by-one with a point on the end and push this firmly into each planting hole, making sure it is straight and secure. These stakes can be used year after year and so are worth investing in. Then take a litre plastic water bottle and cut off the end and push the bottle neck into the planting hole; this makes watering easier as the water gets down to the roots of the plants without wasting any. Finally, cover the membrane with some bark chippings to stop any weeds or the wind doing any damage to the membrane; you may also need to peg it down with wire to stop it blowing away. The bed is now ready for planting. This method can also be used for bush types but they will only need a short stake of about 0.5metre (1ft 6in) and the spacing will need to be about 30–90cm (12–36in), depending on the variety, with the row spacing for bush varieties 90cm (36in), the same as the cordon types. Once you have prepared your bed, you are ready for planting out.

For the glasshouse types, if you have soil in your greenhouse remove the top few centimetres and add a couple of new bags of multi-purpose compost as well as some well-rotted manure or garden compost. Space the tomato plants as for outside, using stakes to support them. You can also use pots if there is no soil in your greenhouse or growbags. Old tyres also make good containers, or you can use old olive oil cans (the kind used in restaurants) with the bottom removed. It is a good idea to plant tagetes and basil around the greenhouse types to ward off pests. It is very important to space them correctly to prevent the numerous pests and diseases that attack greenhouse plants.

Sowing and planting

There is no point in sowing your tomatoes more than eight weeks before the last frost is predicted. If you sow them before this they will be too big to plant out before the danger of frost is past. You can either sow them on the windowsill or in a heated propagator as warm conditions of 15–30°C (59–86°F) are necessary for germination. Sow three seeds to a pot of multi-purpose compost and cover the seeds with vermiculite or sieved compost. After they have germinated, prick them out into individual 5–8cm (2–3in) pots and grow them on in conditions that will provide a temperature of 21–27°C (70–81°F). If you are growing your tomato plants on a windowsill, make sure you turn them every day so they receive equal amounts of light; if not, they will become elongated and difficult to grow on.

Plant them out into their final positions, either in a greenhouse or outside, when danger of frost has passed. They should be about 15cm (1ft) tall at this stage, and their roots should have filled the pot and the first flower buds appeared. Another good tip is to grow them on 'hard' – in other words do not mollycoddle them too much as this will make them more prone to pest and diseases. When you have planted them out, then you can start to pamper them with lots of food and water!

These days many garden centres and nurseries sell tomato plants if you don't want to bother to sow your own. Plant one tomato plant at each stake with a trowel and water in well.

*Tomatoes ripening
on the vine.*

Cultivation

Your tomatoes will need tying in at regular intervals as they grow. Use soft twine or Flexitye. Remember to tie once round the cane and then twist the tie before tying in the tomato, making a figure of eight. In this way you will not damage the stem as it will not rub. Cover bush tomatoes with fleece or cloches and put straw underneath them in June to keep the fruits off the ground. You will need to remove all the sideshoots (that is the shoot that is growing in the leaf axil) in the height of the growing season. You will need to do this almost every day from the cordon varieties. This is not necessary with the bush types, however.

Water the plants daily in the summer and feed them with a liquid high potash fertilizer once a fortnight as soon as the little green fruits begin to swell. Container plants may need to be watered twice a day in dry spells. However, if you overfeed or overwater them, they may lose their flavour and be more prone to pests or diseases. Try to remember to water them at the same time each day – this will help to prevent splitting and other diseases. It is not usual for more than four to five trusses (a collection of fruits) to ripen outside before the first frosts, so pinch out the terminal shoot (the central shoot), leaving just two leaves above the final truss. As the fruits start to ripen, remove the lower leaves to allow the air circulation and to reduce disease, but don't take off too many or any of the higher leaves as this will lead to poor flavour and disease. Hose down the paths in the greenhouse regularly as well as watering to keep red spider mite infestations down.

Harvesting

It is better to allow the tomatoes to ripen on the vine and pick them when they have developed their full colour and a good flavour. At the end of the season you can pick the green tomatoes and either use them for green tomato chutney or put them in a warm place to ripen. You can also hang banana skins in the greenhouse as they give off ethylene gas which aids ripening. Or you can pull up the whole vine and hang it upside down in a warm place indoors to ripen the green fruit. With the outdoor tomatoes, untie them and lay them down on a bed of straw and place cloches over them to aid ripening.

Common problems

Unfortunately tomatoes can have a lot of problems. Outdoor tomatoes are usually trouble-free, but being in the same family as potatoes, they do share several pests and diseases, such as blight and eelworm. This is why crop rotation is very important and you should never grow your tomatoes on land that has had potatoes on it. If the ground is damp, problems may occur with root rot.

Growing tomatoes in growbags will prevent some soil-borne problems. Greenhouse tomatoes tend to suffer from white fly so put up some yellow sticky fly traps so you can take the appropriate action when you notice the flies. Caterpillars, aphids and red spider mite can also be a problem. Irregular watering may cause blossom end rot and splitting.

Turnips: Brassica rapa (Rapifera group)

Life cycle: Hardy biennial.
Site and soil: Sunny, very sheltered spot with rich, but not freshly-manured, soil.
Sow: Mid-March to early April indoors or in a greenhouse.
Harvest: August and September.
Time before harvesting: Twenty to twenty-four weeks.
How many? 500–750g (1-1½lb) roots per 3m (10ft) row.

Turnips are in the brassica family and are biennials usually grown as annuals. They are a fast-growing crop and you can eat the roots or the tasty leaves which will give you spring greens. The taste of turnips is rather an acquired one, but they are delicious if eaten when they are small.

Varieties

'Primera' has good yields of flat-topped roots which have purple tops and attractive smooth skin, best eaten small and fresh. For the early sowings under cloches, use 'Purple Top Milan' or 'Snowball'. 'Oasis' is also good for its early crop of conical white turnips.

Site and soil

The turnip prefers a cool climate and needs lots of rain in an open sunny site. It needs a reasonably fertile soil that has been dug with organic matter added for the previous crop. It may be necessary to apply lime if the soil is acid and then work some general-purpose fertilizer into the ground a week before planting.

Sowing and planting

Turnips really need to be sown directly into the soil as they do not like being transplanted, although it is possible to do if you grow them in modules. They like to be grown quickly and so poor soils are no good. Sow the seeds thinly in 1cm (½in) deep drills spaced 23cm (9in) apart for the early crops and 30cm (1ft) apart for the later ones as they will produce more top growth. Thin the seedlings to 10cm (4in) apart so that the roots can swell.

Cultivation

Keep your crop well watered, especially in dry weather; if not, the turnips will grow in an irregular shape and the roots will split. Keep them well weeded.

Harvesting

They will be ready in about six to ten weeks, depending on the variety. They are not hardy, so lift them before it gets too cold when they reach the size of a golf ball. Cut the leaves as you need them and then more will sprout from the cut stump.

Common problems

Flea beetle may make small holes in the leaves. Possible diseases include mildew and clubroot. Crop rotation is important.

Turnip tops can be used as salad vegetables.

CHAPTER 6

Flowers for cutting

Having a section on your allotment for a cutting garden is a must. Just think of all the wonderful flowers you can have all year round and the money you can save on buying cut flowers for the house. It is a really good way of maximizing the space on your allotment throughout the year and is also an incentive to get outdoors in all weathers. There is nothing better than coming home with armfuls of flowers, both for your house and to give to friends. In short, using your allotments to grow flowers as well as vegetables involves low costs but high returns.

This chapter suggests ways in which you can have cut flowers all year round and recommends different types of flowers to grow.

CHOOSING YOUR SITE

You will need an area roughly 3 x 4.5m in a sunny part of the allotment, preferably in sheltered position away from overhanging trees. Begin by assessing the area you are thinking of using to grow your cut flowers and note how much sunlight it gets. Check for frost patterns and also wind. Don't forget that shade delays seed germination, and wind and shade together will decrease your plant growth. Shelter is important because flower stems are very easily snapped by high winds and damage is soon done to the plants in really windy or wet weather.

Many allotments are on exposed sites, so think about creating a microclimate for your cut flower bed. A good windbreak will protect over a distance of at least eight times its height. Jerusalem artichokes (*see* page 64) could be used as a windbreak,

Just think of all those cut flowers you can have all the year round to bring into the house!

Anemone sp. *is a great plant for growing in the shade.*

as could old pallets joined together. Hurdles look wonderful and do a great job, but they may not be readily available; it's worth contacting a local woodland conservation group to see if they could supply them. Alternatively you could use hardwood cuttings to make a hedge round the area.

PLANNING YOUR SITE

Begin by drawing out a plan for your cutting garden. A really simple plan might be four raised beds with paths between them. Another would be to have a circular bed in the middle for growing your climbers with other beds radiating out for the rest of the flowers. Remember that geometric shapes are much easier to work with than curves; curves are much harder to maintain and are not as accessible for collecting the flowers.

It is important to include paths to allow you access to your flowers. Straw can be useful to make

MAKING A HEDGE FROM HARDWOOD CUTTINGS

First prepare the area for your hedge by making sure it is weed-free. Put down some black polythene or a weed-suppressing membrane to keep the area clear. Although this is quite time-consuming, it will be worth it in the long run to save your hedge from being overtaken by weeds.

Hardwood cuttings can be taken from deciduous shrubs in winter once they have lost their leaves. They should be taken from one-year-old growth and should be pencil-thick and around 25cm in length. Trim the cuttings from beneath a node.

Dig a V-shaped trench, the back of which is vertical, then insert the cuttings to a depth of half or two-thirds their length, about 30cm apart. Keep them well-watered and free from weeds while the hedge establishes itself. Suggested plants for making a hedge include *cornus* (dogwood), *forsythia*, roses and *philadephus* (mock orange).

paths as it can be dug in at the end of the season and will bulk up the structure of the soil. However, it is important to keep the paths clear of weeds as these can easily stray onto the plants. Taking time in careful design and construction of your path is a worthwhile investment.

Once you have marked out your area and provided some kind of windbreak, dig over the soil and add as much garden compost as possible. This is a good area of the allotment to use up some of your homemade compost (*see* page 44); using manure will cause too much green growth and fewer flowers, and some of the hardy annuals prefer poor soil.

FLOWERING PLANTS AND THEIR LIFE CYCLES

It is important to be aware of the life cycles of the plants that will grow throughout the year in your cutting area.

Flowers grown in rows make picking easier.

Herbaceous Perennials

Herbaceous perennials have a life cycle of more than two years. Perennials flower and die back in the winter, although some of them are evergreen, such as some varieties of euphorbia and helleborus. This group is not as prolific in their flowering as annuals, but they can occasionally be used in the house as fillers with other flowers, so it can be useful to grow some in your cutting garden.

Annuals and biennials are generally 'cut-and-come-again', i.e. they only stop producing flowers when they go to seed or when they have finished flowering at the end of the season. The cut-and-come-again method is similar to deadheading annuals, in that when you pick the flowers the plants produce more as their aim is to make as much seed as possible. So, in other words, if you keep picking them they keep reproducing. However, most perennials do not do this, and so it is important to be aware that once you have picked a stem of an agapanthus or iris, for example, it will not flower again.

Hardy Annuals

Hardy annuals generally withstand frosts and are very easy to grow. They form a very important part of the cut flower garden; without them, your garden would be half empty. They can be sown straight into the ground outside from the middle of spring and will germinate and start growing long before the frosts have finished in May.

If you want an early crop in May, it's a good idea to sow in March. However, at this stage of the year, the soil in the garden is too cold and wet for decent rates of germination, so it is best to sow them inside as you would a half-hardy annual (see below). I do this in module trays, which avoids disturbing the roots when they are planted out. Hardy annuals can also be sown in the autumn and planted out for early flowering; however, they can be difficult to look after during the winter months, and I find they are much better sown in the spring.

Hardy annuals can be planted out in rows, but remember to give them plenty of space. I use a 30cm ruler as a guide when planting them out. If you plant them too closely together you will find

Nigella *gives two seasons of interest – first the flowers and then the seed heads.*

that they do not flower well. To appreciate this you only need to look at self-seeded love-in-a-mist (*Nigella*), which grows like mustard and cress but doesn't flower well. However, if you space them out well you will get really good flowers. When you pick them, make sure you take out the centre stem first; this will stimulate side shoots, which will give you flowers for weeks on end.

Half-hardy Annuals

Half-hardy annuals only live for one year. They need heat to germinate and they are unable to tolerate frost and usually die off at the end of the season. However, they are very fast growing and

HERBACEOUS PERENNIALS

These hardy herbaceous perennials will provide continuity of display throughout the season.

- *Iris unguicularis* 'Walter Butt' (used to be known as *Iris stylosa*) is a free-flowering variety which produces scented, pale lavender flowers in winter, up to 7.5cm across. It begins to flower in October or November and continues during mild periods through the winter until March. Foliage may be trimmed back in autumn before flowering starts as it can become messy. It needs to be baked by the sun in summer, so should be planted in a sunny dry location. It also requires shelter from cold winds in winter. The bottom of a south-facing wall is an ideal location. It grows up to 25cm (10in) in height.
- *Viola odorata* 'Czar' (sweet violet) grows 10–15cm (4–6in) high, so is suitable for the front of the border. It grows best in shade and will tolerate dry areas. It has heart-shaped leaves and produces sweetly-scented purple flowers from February to April, and again in the autumn.
- *Pulmonaria officinalis* 'Sissinghurst White' produces brilliant white flowers for weeks in March to May, followed by green leaves marbled with white. Its height is 25cm (10in), and its spread is 45cm (18in). It prefers some shade, as do all the *pulmonarias* (lungworts).
- *Bergenia* 'Bressingham Ruby' has glossy green leaves that turn maroon in winter and hence provide winter interest. It has spikes of deep rose-red flowers in April, and a height and spread of about 35cm (14in), providing good ground cover. It likes sun or partial shade.
- *Doronicum plantagineum* (leopard's bane) has large yellow daisy-like flowers from around April to June, with low clusters of bright green, heart-shaped, hairy leaves. It grows 60cm–1m (2–3ft) high, and may need some support. Slugs like the young leaves, but otherwise it is easy to grow. It should be deadheaded regularly to maintain the flowering period, and likes sun or partial shade.
- *Lupinus* 'The Governor' grows up to 1m tall flower spikes of blue and white, consisting of sweet-pea-shaped flowers, with palmate green

Helenium *'Moerheim Beauty' is a glorious late flowering perennial suitable for cutting.*

leaves. It flowers from June to July, with a second flush later if deadheaded. Quick-growing but short-lived, it likes sun or partial shade. It is prone to mildew and slug damage.

- *Delphinium* 'Black Knight' is about 1.5m (5ft) tall (although some varieties are smaller) with 60cm (2ft) spread, and is ideal for the back of the border, with deep violet-blue flowers with black eyes, borne in dense tall spikes. Its main flowering period is June to July. It needs a sunny site sheltered from strong wind, and tall varieties like this one need staking. Although prone to fungal diseases, it is well worth all the trouble; these are marvellous plants and will come back again if you cut them back after the first flush.
- *Helenium autumnale* 'Moerheim Beauty' has bronze red daisy-type flowers with a prominent central brown disc from July to September. It responds to cutting back by giving a second flush on the side shoots. It is about 1m (3ft) tall, and may need some support in an exposed site, and requires deadheading. It likes sun or partial shade, and needs regular lifting and dividing to maintain flower quality.
- *Anemone japonica* 'Queen Charlotte' (Japanese anemone) is about 80cm (2ft 8in) high with semi-double pink flowers and central gold stamens. Many Japanese anemones have single flowers, and some double. There are some lovely white forms. They flower from August until the first frosts in October. They will tolerate sun or shade. Although they are slow to establish, they soon spread.
- *Aster novi-belgii* 'Ada Ballard' (Michaelmas daisy) is about 1m (3ft) high with lavender blue flowers from September to October. It is very prone to mildew and needs staking.

Others that can be grown as perennials in the cutting garden include *Cynara carunculous*, *Eringium planum*, euphorbia varieties, *Lysimachia atropupurea*, *Paeonia lactiflora*, and also many grasses. A good one is *Stipa gigantean*, which grows to 1.5m (5ft) or more.

Cleome will give spectacular blooms if sown under glass in April.

make excellent cut flowers. To be able to grow these plants you will need either to have a propagator to provide heat for good germination (20°C/68°F is a good guide), or buy plug plants (plants already germinated and grown on to small plants) from a garden centre or by mail order. It is also possible to germinate plants in an airing cupboard, but as soon as they develop leaves, they need to be taken out to give them light to photosynthesize. This can save money on heating bills and time, and also reduce waste as it is all too easy to sow far more than you need. The first thing to remember is not to sow too early. A good guide is to look at your allotment and see when the first weeds start to grow; that shows that the soil is warming up and then is a good time to make a start. This is usually around mid-March to early April.

If you are going to germinate seeds yourself, make sure that you turn the seedlings round every day; if not, the plants will become leggy very quickly. It takes about six weeks from sowing to planting out, depending on the plant, but make sure you time it so that all danger of frost will be past when it comes to planting out. Germinate the seeds in a warm environment; you can use an airing cupboard if you don't have a propagator. Cover the pots with polythene, then as soon as the plants have germinated, put them into a place where they get as much light as possible. I sow all my seeds in module trays as this makes it easy to transplant the seedlings either directly into the soil or to pot them on without too much root disturbance. Make sure

The following plants all make fantastic cut flowers and will give you masses of blooms throughout the season.

- *Centaureas cyanus* (cornflower)
- *Ammi majus* (bishop's flower)
- *Consolida var.* (larkspur)
- *Calendula officinalis* (pot marigold)
- *Escholcholzia californica* (Californian poppy)
- *Helianthus annus* (sunflower)
- *Nigella damascena* (love-in-a-mist)
- *Scabiosa atropupurea* (pincushion flower)

Digitalis purpurea *(foxglove) likes to grow in the shade, and is a delight in early summer.*

that the plants do not get too leggy before potting them on. You can then put them into a greenhouse, cold frame or polytunnel to grow on when the weather gets warmer, making sure you keep an eye on the weather. Cover them with horticultural fleece (a white light protective material) or newspaper if the temperature drops. Ensure good ventilation to avoid damping-off disease or other fungal problems.

When all danger of frost has passed, plant them out into the cut flower area of your allotment. Pinch out the tops if the plant is too leggy, as this will encourage bushy growth from below, making more stems to cut.

Biennials

Biennials have a long flowering season and often produce flowers for an early display. I think they are fantastic as cut flowers as they also often set seed, giving you plenty of blooms year after year.

If you've ever grown biennials, you may well have found they can sometimes live longer than two years. The fact is that most of the plants that we think of as biennials, such as foxgloves and wall-flowers, are actually short-lived perennials. They bulk up in their first year, flower in their second, then usually fizzle out, at which point it is best to pull them up. So, although they are not naturally biennial, they are best grown as such. In the right

spot, however, they may actually thrive for more than two years, hence the confusion. Some biennials, for example wallflowers, become old and woody after a while. I quite like it when they look like this but some people like to grow them from scratch each year.

These half-hardy annuals are recommended for growing in the cut flower area of your allotment.

- *Nicotiana sylvestis* (tobacco plant)
- *Moluccella laevis* (bells of Ireland)
- *Cosmos bipinnatus*
- *Zinnia elegans*
- *Antirrhinum* (snapdragon)
- *Cleome hassle riana* (American spider flower)

Eryngium sp. self-sets freely and gives plenty of cut flowers that can also be dried.

On the other hand, some plants sold as biennials, such as *Angelica archangelica* and *Meconopsis napaulensis* don't always flower in their second year. These plants are monocarpic – that is, like biennials, they flower only once, having spent time producing foliage and maybe taking two or three years before they flower.

Biennials are commonly sold as young plants, usually in autumn, to flower the following summer. Allow them to self-seed and you need never buy them again. Whatever you do, don't buy biennials that are already in flower as they will soon die.

However, you might prefer to grow your own plants from seed, which is very straightforward as most biennials germinate readily. Sow the seeds from late April to July, either in trays or directly in the ground outside where you want them to flower. Water, feed and thin them as required and they will flower the following year. If, however, you don't want to use border space for plants that take a while to flower, sow them in a spare patch of ground

BIENNIALS

These biennials are suitable for your allotment flower garden.

- *Oenothera biennis* (evening primrose)
- *Euphorbia lathyris*
- *Papaver nudicale* (Iceland poppy)
- *Scabiosa atropurpurea*
- *Eryngium giganteum*
- *Campanula medium*
- *Digitalis purpurea* (foxglove)
- *Verbascum bombyciferum*
- *Onopordum acanthium* (Scotch thistle)
- *Myosotis sylvatica* (forget-me-not)
- *Erysimum cheiri* (wallflower)
- *Lunaria annua* (honesty)
- *Alcea officinalis* (hollyhock)
- *Matthiola incana* (sea stock)
- *Dianthis barbatus* (sweet William)
- *Hesperis matronalis* (sweet rocket)

Oenothera biennis *(evening primrose) shines out in*
the twilight.

somewhere out of sight. You can then transplant
them into their final flowering position in the
autumn.

Bulbs

Bulbs are easy to grow, come up year after year, are
cheap and make great cut flowers. They are essen-
tially underground swollen storage organs. When
planting them out, make sure that the basal plate
(the part where the roots come from) is going down
and the pointed end is going up.

Spring bulbs

Spring bulbs need to be planted in the autumn.
With careful planning, you can have a continuity of
colour throughout spring with a variety of bulbs.
The best way to buy them is in bulk by mail order;

that way you can either share them with other allotmenteers or plant them out in large quantities,
which makes them good for cutting. Bulbs bought
by mail order are usually in better condition than
those from a garden centre, where they are usually
kept in excessively hot conditions. Make sure that
the bulbs are healthy; they should be firm and not
covered in mould, with their tunics (the outer
papery skin) intact.

There are numerous varieties of spring bulbs.
Starting with aconites, followed by *galanthus*
(snowdrops), crocus, anemones, fritillaries, hyacinths, narcissus, and then finally tulips, you can get
a wonderful display for very little that will come up
year after year.

The best time to plant your spring bulbs (with
the exception of tulips) is from September to
October. The reason for this is that in order to
flower well, bulbs need to get a good root system
established. It is quite possible to plant spring bulbs
as late as January, but they are not likely to flower
that year as they will be quite weak plants. Tulips,
on the other hand, are best left until November as
they are not ready to start getting established until
then; they also benefit from the cold weather, which
helps to protect them from diseases.

I try to interplant my bulbs with other spring
flowers, such as forget-me-nots and wallflowers;
this method allows you to be sure of where you
have planted them. Alternatively, plant them in lines
or clumps so that you know where they are. They
are also easier to plant that way. Just dig out a
trench at least twice the depth of a bulb and put
each one in. I put them quite close together so they
really give a good display. When you plant your
bulbs, it is a good idea to scatter some bone meal in
the planting hole; this contains phosphorus, which
aids root development. Don't forget that some
bulbs, such as lilies, can do with a bit of grit to help
with drainage if you are on a very heavy soil.

Tulips are best planted a bit deeper than other
bulbs. This stops the bulb from reproducing, making it more likely to come up in the following year;
if not, you will need to plant new bulbs each year.

When your bulbs have died down, make sure
you leave the foliage on for six weeks, thus allowing
energy from the leaves in the form of nutrients to
go back into the bulb, giving it energy to flower

Gladioli have been a traditional allotment flower for generations.

next year. Tying the stems up is not really necessary and furthermore hampers photosynthesis.

Summer bulbs

Summer flowering varieties include alliums, lilies and gladioli, all of which make brilliant cut flowers. Dahlias are tubers rather than bulbs, but often they are included in general descriptions of summer bulbs. Alliums can be planted in the autumn, along with the other bulbs. Lilies can be planted at any time, from autumn to early spring. However, be careful when planting them as they do not have a protective tunic like most bulbs, and so can easily be damaged. They are also prone to rotting in heavy soils, so when planting lilies remember to put some horticultural grit into the planting hole to aid drainage. If they have already started to sprout don't worry, just make sure the shoot is just above the soil and take care not to snap it.

The hybrid gladioli tend to be more tender than the species ones and so they should be planted out

Dahlias will give you cut flowers from June until the first frost.

in rows again in the allotment. You can always use a lettuce or radish crop as a marker to show you where the bulbs have been planted. They make great cut flowers and I always stagger the planting, putting a few in every couple of weeks. Try to leave some of the stem behind when picking; this will give them a good start for the following year as it will allow the bulb to be able to store plenty of food. If you have recently burnt any wood, give them a feed with the potassium-rich ash as this will help future growth; if you don't have ash available, use a high-potassium feed.

Alliums are really good value as not only do you have the blooms but also the seed heads, which provide plenty of interest throughout the rest of the year and also provide food for birds and insects. There are many different types, large and small, and if you mix them together they can make a magnificent display during June. I always plant them closer together than the books generally advise as this makes more of an impact.

Dahlias are the most rewarding of the 'bulb' varieties. It can be possible to begin picking the flowers in June and continue right through to the end of October; that is, if you deadhead them frequently and give them protection from slugs, snails and earwigs. Depending on the weather and where you live, you can leave them outside over winter, certainly in the south of England and probably further north if you use a good mulch as a winter duvet. There are hundreds of different types of dahlias to choose from, so it is worth spending some time on winter nights poring over the catalogues and selecting your varieties. I really like the dark cacti types but the pom-pom dahlias are very popular for cutting as well. Dahlias are cheap if you buy them mail order; they will arrive looking like dried-out sausages, and you may find it hard to believe that they will turn into beautiful flowers – but they will if you give them plenty of food and water.

Growing dahlias has been an allotment tradition for many years and you may well be given lots of conflicting advice from some of the 'experts' on your site! However, it is important to remember that they are very hungry plants and so it is well worth digging in lots of manure before you plant them out. Again, try to plant lots for full effect. Make sure you space them about 60–90cm (2–3ft) apart as they need a lot of room.

STAKING

It is essential to stake dahlias. I always do this when I plant them out in late May, using three stout canes or hazel poles, one at the back and two at the front. Use twine to make two loops around the poles to support them, forming a kind of tepee effect. Lots of cut flowers need staking. You can use pea and bean netting stretched between canes when the plants are very small. Alternatively single canes can be used for tall varieties. Sometimes you can use different varieties of plants to support each other; it really depends on how windy and exposed your site is.

Dahlias are prone to attack by earwigs; use an upturned flowerpot stuffed with straw to trap them in, but be sure to empty the flowerpot every few days. This is all a bit of a process but well worth it for the results. Deadhead your dahlias regularly; if you are confused about what exactly to deadhead, the pointed bits are dead, whereas the round bits are buds that are waiting to come out. When the cold weather begins, dahlias will die back and if there is a frost they may become blackened by it. At this point, cut them down to the ground and cover them with a mulch.

CHAPTER 7

Fruit

Fruit is an excellent crop for the allotment gardener; not only does it provide food, but it is also very ornamental. Both fruit trees and bushes are very attractive and provide a lot of interest throughout the year with their blossom and structure – plus, of course, luscious fruits.

LOCATION

Try to find a sunny position for your fruit. All fruits need the sun to ripen them and to produce a good crop. Also, be aware that areas prone to high rainfall will present problems such as scab on apples and pears, leaf spot on currants, rotting of stone fruits and grey moulds. Try to avoid planting fruit in low-lying areas where frost pockets occur as frost can cause damage to the flowers, therefore destroying any cropping possibilities.

- A south-facing aspect provides the most warmth for the longest time during the day, and any fruit will grow here.
- A west-facing aspect is still warm and will get the afternoon sun, and will be fine for all fruits except figs and apricots.
- East-facing aspects receive the morning sun, but don't forget the soil will be dry and may need additional watering in the summer.
- A north-facing aspect, being the coldest, is suitable for gooseberries and red and white currants.

*Try growing something unusual, like quince (*Cydonia)*, which is fully hardy.*

TYPES OF FRUIT

It is important to understand the terms that are used when fruit is discussed. These are some of the most common terms you will encounter.

- Tree fruit or top fruit: this refers to, for example, apples, pears and plums or trees that are grown in the open ground in a natural way. The term used to describe these trees is *unrestricted*, and when trees are trained in a way to make them more compact they are known as *restricted* forms, for example cordons, pyramid, fan or espalier.
- Bush fruits: these are such fruit as gooseberries, blackcurrants, blueberries, and red and white currants.
- Cane fruit: this refers to fruit that grows on canes, for example raspberries, loganberries and blackberries. These usually require support.
- Finally there are strawberries; these are perennial plants and you can use the alpine variety for edging or the ordinary kind for growing in beds.

PREPARING THE SITE

The most important thing about successfully growing fruit is to make sure you prepare the site well. It really is worth taking time and trouble with this as it is an area that can quickly be overtaken by weeds and you can soon become demoralized by it.

A fruit cage will deter all sorts of pests.

Firstly you will need quite a large area of your allotment. Even bush fruits need plenty of space as they will soon get lots of pests and diseases if they are restricted. Of course, you can include fruit bushes in the flower borders as some of them make very attractive specimens; blueberries in particular provide the most fantastic autumn colour.

Before siting your fruit area, there are a few things to consider. Firstly, make sure that the soil is well prepared. Ensure that all weeds have been carefully removed and that you add plenty of organic matter. Fruit needs free-draining soil as badly drained soil can lead to the roots not developing properly, which in turn will lead to diseases. You can then lay a permeable membrane over the ground, mark out where you will put your fruit, allowing plenty of space for each one. Cut a cross in the membrane where the fruit is to go and, after planting and watering in well, use bark chippings to weigh down the membrane. That way weeds can be kept to a minimum. The soil should be between 45 and 60cm (18in–3ft) deep. Slightly acid soil is preferable and shallow soils over chalk will give rise to problems such as lime-induced chlorosis.

Tree fruits should not need to be watered after they are established, if you prepare and feed the ground well, except in periods of drought. Soft fruit needs more water as the roots are near the surface. When the fruit is being formed is the most important time for watering for all types of fruit. Apply a balanced fertilizer in the spring and mulch with grass clippings and wood ash; the wood ash provides potassium, which will help with plant health and fine fruits and also help with winter hardiness. However, do not overfeed with nitrogen, e.g. grass clippings, as it will give too much vegetative growth; consequently nitrogen is best applied in the spring.

If you think this is all a lot to remember, keeping an allotment diary will really help you in your first few years of gardening to make sure you know exactly what to do and when. I also like to refer to month-by-month guides in horticulture books to jog my memory on what to do. A suggested calendar of allotment tasks is given on page 155. Some things will come naturally after a while but others may take longer.

SOFT FRUIT

The first thing to consider when growing fruit bushes is to make sure that you offer some protection from the birds – if not, you will find they will end up eating more than you do. Bullfinches and sparrows will eat the buds in winter, and then blackbirds and pigeons will be after the fruits in summer. It is possible to net bushes individually, but this is such a time-consuming process that it is much better to cover the whole area if you can. There are various methods you can use, such as putting old plastic bottles or flower pots over the top ends of canes pushed into the earth, then draping netting over the top. The best way is to make or buy a fruit cage that you can walk into – you could build a frame for this using old pallets. You only have to walk around a few allotment sites to see masses of innovative styles of fruit protection!

Raspberries

Raspberries will grow almost anywhere, provided they are planted on well-drained soil. They can continue producing fruit for up to ten to twelve years. There are two types of raspberry – summer fruiting and autumn fruiting. It is easy to get the two muddled up and therefore it is best to grow them in two very different places. The reason for this is that they require two different types of pruning. You should get a yield of up to 900g (2lb) per 30cm (1ft) run of row for summer-fruiters and about 225g (½ lb) for autumn-fruiters. These fruits are great for growing on allotments; they are good to pick on a summer's day and have so many uses. In your first couple of years, aim to grow just enough fruit to make summer pudding – marvellous!

Summer fruiting

Summer fruiting types are easily recognized as they branch out and the old fruit stalk can be seen.

Raspberries – keep the summer and autumn fruiting canes separate.

Summer fruiting canes produce their fruit on canes grown the previous year. After fruiting in July to August, any weak canes should be cut to the ground, leaving only the strongest of the new canes.

These fruits need support and one way of growing them is around the perimeter of the allotment trained against some kind of support. You could make this using 2m (7½ft)-long posts, pushed .5m (18in) into the ground at 3.5–4.5m (12–15ft) intervals. Stretch Gauge 14 galvanized wires between the posts at .5, 1 and 1.5m (2½, 3½ and 5½ ft). Grown like this, the fruits will look beautiful when both fruiting and flowering. Another way of supporting them is to drive 2.5m (7½ ft) long posts .5m (18in) into the ground and plant four canes around each post.

Blackberries can be trained over a greenhouse to provide shade in the summer.

The best time to plant summer fruiting raspberries is between November and March. It is best to buy them mail order from a reputable grower. One of the reasons for buying them in this way is that you will get virus-free certified stock.

Soak the canes in a bucket of water before planting. Prepare the ground well; digging a trench is the easiest way, incorporating plenty of well-rotted manure. The canes should be planted about 40 cm (1½ ft) apart. They don't need to be planted too deeply, about 8cm (3in) of soil is enough. A week before planting it is best to rake in a couple of handfuls of fish blood and bone along the row. After planting, cut the canes back to 30cm (1ft); although this seems harsh, it will really help the plants establish themselves quicker. 'Glen Moy' and 'Malling Jewel' are recommended varieties with a good flavour and some disease resistance.

Autumn Fruiting

Autumn fruiting raspberries bear fruit in midsummer on the previous season's growth in the normal way, but also produce flowers on the new canes. This fruit ripens from mid-August onwards and sometimes as late as October or November. It is the easiest fruit to prune as all you have to do each winter is to cut the canes down to ground level and up they come again the next year. Nothing could be simpler. Good varieties are 'Autumn Bliss' and 'Terri-Louise'.

Blackberries and hybrid berries

These are also cane fruits and need some kind of support. They can be trained over an arch and together, with loganberries (crosses between raspberries and blackberries), are great for providing shade over the greenhouse during the summer months. All you need to do is remove the canes once they have fruited on previous and current season's growth, and cut them down to the ground. Tie the new canes either to a support, over an arch or to the front of the greenhouse. 'Veronique' is a new compact pink-flowering thornless variety to look out for and 'Silvan' has a high level of disease resistance.

Redcurrants and whitecurrants

These are the jewels of the fruit garden, and look so beautiful sparkling in the sunshine. Having said that, they are also quite tolerant of shade and will grow quite happily against a north-facing fence. You can grow them as fans, cordons or standards, which is very helpful if space is limited. It is usual to buy a two- or three-year-old bush. They can cope better than blackcurrants on a poor soil but it is still best to give them a good start by improving the soil and feeding and mulching them annually. Plant them 1.5m (5ft) apart. They are closely related to gooseberries and should be pruned in the same way. It is important to encourage side shoots to form. This is best done at planting time. Any crossing shoots should be shortened to two buds of the main stem. After that all you need to do is to cut back one of the main branches to a bud just above ground level once a year. Give them some potash in January and mulch them with organic matter and they will reward you with redcurrants to make your

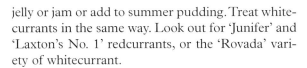
Redcurrants hang like jewels in the sunshine.

Gooseberries can be grown on a single stem to save space.

jelly or jam or add to summer pudding. Treat white-currants in the same way. Look out for 'Junifer' and 'Laxton's No. 1' redcurrants, or the 'Rovada' variety of whitecurrant.

Gooseberries

These are the first fruit of the season, and are both easy to grow and very hardy. These fruits have a permanent branch structure. It is possible to grow them as a cordon or fan and you can also train them into double to triple cordons. If you are making cordons, plant them 50cm apart and 1.5m between the rows. In summer, cut back the new lateral branches to five leaves from their starting point and then in winter cut back the leader to one bud above the previous year's growth when the required height has been reached. Prune back the lateral shoots to one bud. Practise this on an old branch until you are familiar with all the terms.

The good thing about currants and gooseberries is that you can take hardwood cuttings from them in the winter to help you to increase your stock. All you have to do is make cuttings 25cm (10in) long in the winter, plant them in groups of three where you want them to grow and make sure to bury all but the top 5cm (2in). However, do be aware of viruses, and make sure the cuttings are well-watered in the first year. Good varieties to try are 'Careless' and 'May Duke', which is a red variety; these ripen at different times, and can give you up to 4.5kg (10lb) of fruit from one bush. The other good thing about them is that they freeze well and make good preserves.

Blackcurrants

These are as easy to grow and look after. They aren't very fussy about soil, although they are not too keen on thin chalk or anything too acidic, so just

Alpine strawberries make an attractive edging plant.

add the usual organic matter to improve the water-holding ability. Again a gap of 1.5m is needed between each plant. Make sure you plant them a bit deeper than they were in the pot that you bought them in as this will encourage the stems to produce more roots.

Blackcurrants fruit on young wood made the previous year, so it is really important to prune and feed them well. Cut them back to one bud above soil level on planting and then a year later you will have seven or eight strong stems that will bear fruit the following summer. Feed and mulch them every year and try not to prune too early as the birds love to eat the new buds. Winter time is when pruning should be carried out, after the leaves have fallen. Prune out any spindly shoots to ground level, and at the same time remove a few old branches. This will encourage more stems to grow from the base of the plant, but make sure

that you don't remove more than a third of the stems or you will end up with lots of vegetative growth that will be unproductive. Remember that pruning stimulates growth.

Once the bush has established, it should yield around 4.5kg (10lb) of fruit, more than enough to make plenty of delicious pies and smoothies, plus a few bottles of homemade wine.

Strawberries

Strawberries are rather a high-maintenance fruit to grow and you should only attempt to grow them if you have plenty of time to devote to them, otherwise you will be bitterly disappointed. You can grow summer-fruiting varieties for early crops; these usually only crop once in the early summer, and then there are supposedly perpetual strawberries so that you can still be picking them in October. These perpetual varieties have the characteristic of producing fruit in flushes though the summer until the frost comes and then they stop producing.

However, if you put a cloche over them this may well extend the season even more.

Alpine strawberries are good to grow as edging around vegetable and herb beds; they are absolutely delicious, but they never seem to reach the kitchen as everyone picks them as they walk around. When you are harvesting other vegetables, they make a welcome sweet and juicy stop!

Strawberries are best planted in full sun, although they will tolerate dappled shade if they have to. Alpine strawberries are usually grown from seed and kept for not longer than two years.

Viruses are a problem with strawberries and all types should be replaced every three years. Moreover, perpetual types deteriorate after two years so it is best to replant the runners then. In July dig in some well-rotted manure or some garden compost. Just before you plant them, rake in some fertilizer – fish, blood and bone or seaweed would be good – at about 75g (3oz) per square yard. You should then plant the strawberries in July or August or at the latest September so that they establish well; if not, they are unlikely to be much good in the first year and you should remove the flowers. Plant them about 45cm (18in) apart and make sure you spread out the roots, keeping the crowns (where the roots meet with the stems) level with the soil surface to prevent rotting. Make sure you firm them in well.

Make sure you keep them well watered during dry spells and if possible plant them through some kind of permeable membrane to prevent too many weeds building up. When the strawberries begin to swell up, give them some protection from slugs and also woodlice. Cover the ground underneath the berries with straw as this will keep the fruit clean. Use netting supported over cloches to protect them from the birds. You could also try cloches made from wire netting and bent into a tunnel shape; they do the job and look quite good too!

When the strawberry plants have finished fruiting, cut off the leaves and any runners that have not been used for propagation with a pair of shears. This will help to prevent the build-up of pest and diseases. It is best to move your strawberry bed every three years; this will help to prevent the plants becoming sick.

During the third year it is a good idea to propagate your stock during June, July or August when the runners are produced. Select four or five runners from healthy plants. Using a U-shaped wire, peg down the runners into the ground or pots filled with potting compost. In four to six weeks they should have rooted and then you can sever them from the parent plant and plant them out into a new bed and water them in.

TOP FRUIT

Before planting fruit trees, make sure you check with your allotment provider as to whether there are any restrictions as far as height is concerned, as different rules apply to planting trees in different areas.

The first thing to consider when buying a fruit trees is its eventual size. Most fruit trees these days are grafted, which helps to control the vigour of the tree and produce more fruit, as some fruit does not grow very well on its own roots. The grafted-on piece is called the scion and this is grafted onto the rootstock. (This explains how you end up with 'family' apple trees, where several different varieties are grafted onto one rootstock.)

The scion is a shoot from the fruit variety, and the rootstock is the root system that dictates the ultimate size and vigour of the tree. If you don't want a large spreading tree you will need a dwarfing rootstock.

Apples

Apples are a good choice for the allotment gardener as they are very hardy. There is a huge choice of variety and ways of growing them, e.g. cordons, espaliers, fans, bushes or columns. It is also possible to have them cropping from August right through to November if you choose different varieties. The apple rootstocks are known by 'M' or 'MM'; the reason for this is that they were developed at the Malling Fruit Research Station (the M series) or the Merton (MM series). If you want a very vigorous tree then go for MM111, after that comes MM106 which is semi-dwarfing, 11½ ft (3.5m), then M26; this is known as dwarfing rootstock for average soils, and will take three or four years to produce the first fruits, followed by M9 which grows to 6½ft (2m) and again takes three to

Above: Protect pear blossom from spring frosts.

Left: Top fruit trained against an old metal bed post.

four years to crop. M27 is known as extremely dwarfing and the approximate size of the tree is 5ft (1.5m) after ten years; however, it will fruit after two to three years and is suitable for cordons and step-over apples.

It is important to remember that no apple tree is completely self-compatible (i.e. not self-fertile), and needs another apple tree nearby. Fruit trees are pollinated by insects and consequently it is important that two trees must be in flower at the same time for pollination to be successful. For this reason apple trees are divided into groups, Group 1 being the earliest to flower; it is important to choose trees from the same group or either side of the group. A pollination table is helpful when looking for suitable trees. This can be found in a good fruit reference book or on the internet.

It is important to remember that some apples, e.g. Bramleys, are triploid (1.5 times the number of chromosomes); in other words, because they are poor pollinators they need two diploids (normal number of chromosomes) to produce flowers and then eventually fruit. As usual in horticulture, there are exceptions; for instance, the apple 'Crawley Beauty' is in Group 7 and flowers when others have finished, and therefore is able to set its own fruit.

Pears

Pears are also good fruit trees to grow but it is important to remember that they flower earlier than apples and so they need more frost protection and also more sun and warmth during the growing season for the pears to ripen. Pears are grown on quince rootstocks and they are not self-fertile, needing another pollinator nearby.

Plums

These are well worth growing, and there are many different varieties including the dessert Victoria, which produces a heavy crop and makes great jam. Plums also flower early and so it is best to grow them in the south-facing part of the allotment away from cold winds. If you grow plums as bushes, fans or minarettes, they are easier to protect, prune and harvest. You will not have to wait for so long for the fruit either as most of these will fruit after a couple of years.

Plant apple trees on dwarfing rootstocks so they don't create too much shade.

Plums are great for jam-making.

Peaches

Peaches often start to flower as early as February, so make sure that you erect a cover to put over them if there is any danger of frost. The best place to grow them outdoors is against a wall or, in the case of the allotment-holder, a south-facing fence. Because they flower so early, it is a good idea to hand-pollinate them with a soft brush as usually at this time of the year pollinating insects are in short supply. You will need to do it most days when the plant is in flower, but imagine how worthwhile this will be when you eat your first peach!

Pruning of established trees

There are many different ways and times to prune fruit trees and for specifics it is best to refer to a good book on fruit pruning. Spend a bit of time reading it and then use an old branch to practise on; that way you will be sure of the terms used, and how it should be done. It really is worth investing in some good loppers for this job and a sharp pruning saw will also help make the task much easier.

Unpruned trees tend to produce large crops of small fruit, which are often damaged by pests and diseases. If you prune your trees you will improve the air circulation and the light will be able to penetrate and ripen the wood and encourage fruit buds, and also reduce pests and diseases. Pruning is also essential to control the size and shape of the tree or bush to make picking easier. Don't forget that stone fruits (plums, gages, cherries, peaches, nectarines, apricots and sweet almonds) should not be pruned during the dormant season (October–March) because of the risk of silver leaf and bacterial canker infection. It is better to delay pruning of these trees until June.

CHAPTER 8

Allotment enemies

CHALLENGES

In a way this is the most important chapter in this book. Know your allotment enemies and how to deal with them and you will have a great gardening experience; let weeds, pests and diseases get the better of you and it will be far from pleasurable. So read this chapter carefully and try as many of the methods suggested as possible.

There are many challenges for the allotment-holder, including the many pests and diseases that may attack your flowers and vegetables, and threaten your potential produce. There are birds, such as pigeons and bullfinches; mammals, such as rabbits and mice; plus an enormous number of smaller pests, such as slugs, snails, nematode worms, millipedes and mites, etc. Also of course there are diseases, fungi, bacteria and viruses.

Prevention is better than cure

Try to prevent troubles before they start. Check that you have cultivated the ground thoroughly, and that you have removed all perennial weeds before planting as many of these cause pests and diseases. Adding organic matter will help to open up heavy soil that is prone to waterlogging in winter; this is one of the major causes of root-rotting diseases. Organic matter will also help with the water- and food-holding capacity of light soil, helping to prevent pests and diseases.

Make sure you choose the correct plants for the site. Don't grow sun-lovers in a shady spot, and make sure you only pick hardy plants to grow in any areas that are prone to frost. Make sure you buy

Friends and enemies.

Attracting beneficial insects will help with pest control.

good quality plants and bulbs; specialist nurseries are the best places to look for these. Keep an eye out for disease-resistant varieties of plants, many of which are now available to the allotment grower. Make sure you know the soil requirements for your plants and then make sure you plant them properly, ensuring there are no air pockets in the soil, so that the roots will spread into the allotment soil as quickly as possible to support the plant. Remove any weeds and rubbish as these really are a breeding ground for pests.

This collar will prevent the cabbage root fly from laying her eggs in the soil.

Pesticides

All your allotment enemies can be controlled either organically or with pesticides. There are as many pesticides as there are pests. However, there are many disadvantages in using chemicals too freely. Remember that the word pesticide is the umbrella term used to describe insecticides for controlling insects, fungicides for controlling diseases, and herbicides for controlling weeds.

Here are some facts about the use of chemicals to bear in mind when you are considering using pesticides on your allotment.

- Expense. They are expensive especially when used in large areas such as allotments.
- Organisms become resistant and consequently the chemicals have to keep increasing in strength and density.
- Very few chemicals are specific enough; they affect everything they come into contact with, both enemies and friends.
- Fruit crops need bees for pollination – these are harmed by the too generous use of pesticides.

- Unseen animals are killed that usually prey on pests; this will upset the balance of a natural community.
- Chemicals can also contaminate vegetables and time is needed to elapse between spraying and harvesting; this is known as harvest interval.
- The damage spreads through the food chain; birds die as a result of eating smaller animals that have fed on smaller insects.
- Although a great deal of money is spent researching the toxic effects of chemicals there is no doubt that spreading poisons around the countryside has huge implications. Although chemicals are efficient there are several alternatives.

It is important to inform yourself about chemicals so you can make choices about the way you control pests, diseases and weeds. It is not enough to say you are organic without looking into the reasons why. Another thing to consider is that chemicals are constantly being reviewed and taken off the market as new research is carried out, therefore it can be difficult to keep up. For more information on chemicals look on the Department of the Environment, Food and Rural Affairs website (www.defra.gov.uk). It is for many of the reasons stated above that I have chosen to be an organic gardener, and find that if you follow the alternative methods of crop protection listed in this book you should have a harvest enough for your family and friends, and at the same time learn to live with some of the pests that are around; for instance, if the birds eat some of your fruits and you have enough does it really matter?

Natural pest control

Beneficial insects and wildlife are really your best friends when it comes to controlling pests in your allotment. Planting simple annuals amongst your vegetables such as Californian poppies (*Escholtzia*) and marigolds (*Tagetes*) will attract a wealth of beneficial insects like ladybirds and hoverflies who will gobble up your aphids. Plant a few native shrubs and herbaceous perennials (e.g. hazel and hardy geraniums).

Maximizing air circulation by correct pruning and leaving just a little more space between your plants can help to control fungal diseases, for example powdery mildew in roses. If trying to remove a diseased branch from a tree, one with coral spot for example, cut into the healthy wood and always wash your tools in boiling water afterwards. Check your plants regularly so that any pests and diseases don't get a chance to get a hold.

Use your diary to make a note of any pests and disease you see so that you can look out for them next year. For example, if you start checking the centre of your gooseberry bushes in April for sawfly eggs and larvae you can remove them and therefore prevent them defoliating your crop. Also be wary of accepting onion and cabbage plants from your friendly neighbour; they may well carry the dreadful diseases of onion white rot and clubroot. If you have an allotment with either of these diseases, then don't even use the same tools or boots in your garden or you will spread them. Always scrub out your pots and give your greenhouse a good scrub every winter to get rid of those overwintering pests.

Other crop protection methods include cabbage collars made from old carpet. Cut out a circle and make a cut to the centre, then fit this round the base

The carrot fly will bypass a barrier as she will not be attracted by the aroma of the carrot.

of the cabbage or other brassicas. This will prevent eggs from getting into the soil laid by the cabbage root fly. Placing a bottle cloche (a clear plastic drinks bottle with the top and bottom removed) over newly planted vegetables will prevent them being eaten by slugs or anything else that takes a fancy to them.

Barriers are the best way of reducing pest damage. Simply by covering your vegetables with fine mesh you will stop them being attacked by flying pests. This works well for carrot root fly and pea moth. Fine mesh is also an all-inclusive way of protecting your cabbages from just about everything. For example, flea beetles, leaf weevils, birds, cabbage white butterflies and whitefly. If you use a barrier method with slugs remember that success

Galium aparine (sticky willy or cleavers) is easy to weed out if you catch it early.

depends on you being extremely generous with the chosen deterrent and not skimping.

Barriers can also be used to prevent disease. For example peach leaf curl is a devastating fungus that can simply be prevented by placing a barrier of polythene sheeting over a trained peach tree in winter. This barrier prevents the spores splashing up onto the plant.

Another popular method of protecting your plants is to use traps. This can be anything from beer traps for slugs to codling moth traps for you apple trees, or sticky traps for your glasshouse. A codling moth trap, for example, uses a pheromone placed on a sticky floor inside a small tent that is hung in the tree. The male is attracted to the trap as he thinks it is a female. When he lands inside the 'tent' he gets stuck in the glue. You can use similar traps for pear and plum moths. Another good reason for using this method is that you can monitor the number of moths that are around and, when they appear, ready to be on your guard for next

time. Grease bands painted around the trunks of apple trees in autumn are a good way of preventing the wingless female winter moths from climbing up the tree to mate. Sticky glue is also very useful for glasshouse staging if you have an ant problem.

WEEDS

Before we look at weeds it is important to know what a weed is and the difference between annual and perennial weeds; also to make choices about how to treat individual weeds, either organically or by using herbicides.

What is a weed?

The Spanish bluebells in my garden are definitely weeds; I just don't want them there. They produce a huge amount of foliage, look wonderful in April when they are in flower but for the rest of the time are a nightmare! They are difficult to remove and anything else that I happen to have planted is completely overtaken by the bluebells.

You may have noticed a red tulip in your bed of yellow ones; this is equally a weed as it is a plant that is growing in the wrong place. So in other words one person's weed could be another person's much loved plant. Having said this of course, it is usually an excess of a particular type of plant in the wrong place that causes us trouble. In this country we have a selection of weeds that thrive; for example, ground elder, horsetails, couch grass, bindweed, nettle and shepherd's purse, and in lawns clover, dandelion, yarrow, daisy and speedwell – as many as 50,000 seeds per square metre have been recorded. Some weeds have been introduced to this country such as the dreaded Japanese knotweed, speedwell and creeping bellflower, as garden plants. They then became naturalized, either by wind-blown seeds or small pieces of underground stem or rhizome. They are so successful as they have been able to adapt to different soils and situations and some grow strongly under adverse conditions such as lawn weeds which, when mowed frequently, become stronger and reproduce rapidly.

I have now got celandine in my garden as a friend gave me a plant as a present from her garden, obviously with celandine in it; not only do I have to cope with Spanish bluebells in the spring but

Bindweed (Calystegia sepium) flowers look pretty, but it needs to be kept under control.

celandines as well. At least they are both colourful! Garden centres and nurseries are also place where 'new' weeds can be picked up in pots of new plants.

Get to know your weeds; before you do anything else make sure you become familiar with the weeds on your allotment and their life cycles and how they spread. Get a book on wildflowers to identify native weeds, and also sketch or draw weed seedlings when they emerge so you know what they will look like and how to get rid of them. When you are weeding always make sure you have a weed bucket with you. Those colourful plastic trugs are perfect for the allotment gardener; you can have one for weeds, one for compost and one for water. Weeds often get transferred from one place to another on the bottom of people's boots. You only need a tiny piece of bindweed or ground elder stuck on your boot and you could give it to your allotment neighbour forever. So remember always have a weed bucket with you; it is so easy to pull out a weed and forgetfully throw it down on the ground. Remember 'one year's seed seven years' weed' so be aware of spreading seeds of weeds when you are brushing past your plants.

What happens if we just leave weeds, because some of them are very attractive plants, for instance *Geranium robertianum* (herb robert)? First of all they compete for the moisture, nutrients, light, air and growing space with your other crops. Also they can act as host plants for pests and diseases causing viruses. If weeds have grown densely they also harbour pests such as slugs and snails in their foliage.

Annual weeds

Annual weeds include groundsel (*Senecio vulgaris*), hairy bitter cress (*Cardamine hirsute*), chickweed and shepherd's purse; these are all ephemeral weeds, i.e. they can complete up to three life cycles within one year, and for this reason are short lived. Another example of an annual weed is cleavers or goose grass (*Galium aparine*).

Annual weeds complete their life cycle (germinate, grow, flower, set seed and die) within a season. They do not have rhizomes, tubers or bulbils in which to store food so they can survive the winter, but depend on producing seed to survive (groundsel can produce 1,000 seeds per plant). They tend to be more of problem on cultivated ground, as cultivation such as digging tends to bring the seeds to the surface, which aids germination. This is one of the reasons that no-dig beds are thought to be a good method of weed management. The weeds will grow stronger than your crops so it is very important to control these. The best way to do this is to use a hoe; you should try to develop a weeding regime of a few minutes every time you visit the allotment. Just use your hoe and literally knock the tops of the weeds and leave them on the surface to shrivel up in the sunshine. I never put any weeds, not even annual ones, on the compost heap as they are often seeding and unless your compost heap gets really hot they will spread when you put your compost on the beds. The rule is hoe regularly and be very vigilant as they pop up frequently. Get to know them and you will be fine. For more difficult places use a trowel or weeding implement, whichever one suits you best.

Perennial weeds

Perennial weeds are, however, more of a problem. They grow from year to year, survive the winter cold and rear their heads when the soil warms up. They are able to do this as they can store food over winter in their roots, tubers, bulbs or rhizomes. Some examples of these plants are perennial nettles, Japanese knotweed, bindweed, dandelions and oxalis. Blackberries and ground elder are woody stemmed and survive by storing food in their stems and branches. These are usually very prevalent on allotments. When choosing your allotment make sure you check your neighbours' weed situation as there is often nothing to stop weeds spreading from one allotment to another and it can be such a thankless task if you are constantly fighting to control perennial weeds. There are of course chemicals but if you decide to take the organic route try some other methods such as removing the weeds and then covering the ground with membrane.

Remember that if you leave one small piece of stem or root of some of these weeds they will re-grow. Television gardener Geoff Hamilton once famously nailed a dock root to his shed door and two years later took it down and planted it and it still grew!

Raised beds are helpful, as they help to contain the weeds and you will not feel so overwhelmed when it comes to keeping them under control. Remember you have to keep on top of these weeds; if you keep digging them out you will be able to eradicate them eventually.

Try growing *Tagetes minuta*, which is not a garden flower but grown for its root secretions, which are reputed to suppress ground elder and bindweed when planted amongst it. It is a half-hardy annual so start it off on your windowsill early in the year for best results. The strong-smelling foliage is used to repel flies and moths, and this plant is available through the *Organic Gardening Catalogue*. A friend has used it with great success. Also make sure you check all the plants, manure and soil you bring to the allotment for traces of perennial weed stems or roots. Try to remove them with a fork rather than a spade as a spade just chops some of them up and makes even more. Some councils offer to rotivate allotments, but check what weeds you have first as this could be more of a hindrance than a help. Use groundcover where you can in the form of membrane, slabs, bricks on paths and also plants, shrubs and groundcover where there is bare land. Also remember that some plants such as potatoes suppress weeds and others such as onions grow vertically and do not produce much foliage so try to rotate these two crops. Keep on top of the weeds and you will feel able to be in control of your allotment.

Herbicides

Below are some facts about herbicides so you can decide whether it is worth using them or not. I prefer to use alternative methods; there is no such thing as an organic weedkiller and so organic gardeners need to hoe or pull out the weeds! Flame weeders provide an excellent way of removing weeds without resorting to chemicals. Herbicides can be used to:

- Completely clear uncultivated areas of all vegetation.
- Keep hard areas like paths, drives and patios free of weeds.
- Kill weeds within ornamental, vegetable or fruit gardens.
- Kill weeds selectively in lawns.

Different herbicides act in different ways.

Contact herbicides

These are only effective against annual weeds, as these chemicals kill the growth they touch, but not the roots. These weedkillers do not distinguish between weeds and your plants, so take care not to get any on your plant foliage! Home-made shields of cardboard, or an inverted dustbin lid, can be used to protect plants while you're applying chemicals.

Residual (soil acting) herbicides

These are only suitable for use on uncultivated ground, such as pathways, or on bare ground between large, woody plants such as shrubs and trees. These are held in the soil and prevent germination of seeds. They are also used on hard areas to keep them free of weeds. If used on soil the soil must not be disturbed after application.

Systemic herbicides

These are used to combat perennial weeds, as you spray the chemical onto the leaves and the plant then takes the poison right down to the roots. Glyphosate is the most widely available chemical. Apply it on a windless day and shield nearby plants with wood or cardboard, because the weedkiller kills plants too. You can treat perennial weeds that grow among garden plants with this weedkiller in gel form. Either paint the gel onto the leaves, or put on a pair of tough, rubber gloves, smear the weedkiller over the palms, and simply pull the stems through your hands but take care that newly treated weeds don't come into contact with your plants.

Selective herbicides

These will affect certain plants but not others. Lawn weedkillers are in this category, killing broad-leaved weeds but not the grasses.

PESTS

There are a whole host of pests that come in many varieties, the largest variety being insects. It is important to look at the life cycle of some insects, which go through a number of stages from egg to adult. The reason for this is that sometimes the larva (sometimes known as a grub, maggot or caterpillar) can do as much damage as the adult. Some insects such as caterpillars are munching

An old rotary washing line finds a new purpose as a bird-scarer.

insects and chew their way through vegetation and some such as aphids are sap-suckers. It is important to observe how the culprit works to identify who is responsible for the damage.

Many pests are plant-specific; for example Viburnum beetle only appears on Viburnums; for this reason it is impossible to mention them all, but if you have a pest you are unsure of do ask other allotment-holders as often pests colonize one place. Failing that, consult a good pest and disease book (the RHS is always a reliable resource) to check out the problem. If you are an RHS member you can send your pests to them for identification.

Birds

Let's begin with birds; remember that they are protected by law in this country. Bullfinches are a problem from midwinter to spring as they go for the buds of trees, shrubs and soft fruit. Wood pigeons are always on the lookout for a nice lunch of tasty brassica leaves and will really enjoy your pea and bean seeds. They also damage young

Slug damage with the culprit still visible.

seedlings. They are on the go from spring to early summer and really can cause a huge amount of devastation. The best form of defence is to use buzz lines (special tape that is stretched between two posts and makes a buzzing sound) and netting, but make sure that this has very small holes in it as this will stop the cabbage white butterfly and also slugs and snails from attacking your brassicas and other vegetables. Hanging up CDs above your vegetables is another method to try. There is also the potato bird, a potato stuck with feathers, which is supposed to scare the living daylights out of pigeons!

The netting method is my chosen method that seems to work well; I use a hazel pole the length of the bed with willow arches and drape the netting over it and weigh it down at the sides. This makes weeding easy as when you want to weed all you have to do is to roll up the netting on the hazel pole. You may sometimes see starlings pecking at grass areas but they are generally feeding on lawn pests such as leatherjackets and this outweighs any damage they may cause.

Rabbits

Rabbits seem to be a real problem for many allotment-holders and it is so soul-destroying when your crops are completely ruined by rabbits. Because of the nature of the layout of allotments it is particularly difficult to control them. Leafy vegetables are a particular risk and of course they will strip bark from young trees, which can cause the trees to die. Before taking on an allotment, do check about the rabbit problem and find out how the other allotment-owners deal with this issue.

There are several effective control methods. Surround the area with 1.24m (4ft) wire fence sunk 45cm (18in) into the ground angled outwards to stop rabbits from burrowing underneath. Make sure that the gauge is very small, as I have seen baby rabbits squeeze through some wire netting to get to a nice juicy carrot! For individual plants netting 90cm (36inches) high can be put round the plant without the need to bury any underground. Tree guards can be used around young trees to prevent

Slug pellets only need to be used in moderation, unlike this overzealous gardener!

rabbits gnawing the bark. You can also try and grow plants that are more resistant to rabbit attack, around the edge of the plants that rabbits most like! They tend to nibble their way along the edge so this method should help. Try plants with very aromatic leaves, prickles or spines or tough leathery leaves.

Slugs and snails

If I had a pound for every time I have been asked what to do about slugs and snails I would be very rich; they are the bane of the gardener's life. They seem to eat just about everything, including vegetables, herbaceous plants, seeds, bulbs, and of course slugs even enjoy a good feast on main crop potatoes. They are more active at night, especially after a heavy downpour. They leave irregular holes in leaves and other plant parts, and always leave slime trails behind them so it is easy to identify them. I think that one of the biggest attracters of slugs and snails is untidy and unhygienic areas in the allotment, and this is often a problem if you have a neighbour who is not very vigilant. Try not to leave

empty pots around or piles of material for them to hide in.

Raised beds help as you can get old copper pipe from scrap yards and put this round the top of the bed. Petroleum jelly is also a helpful means of defence, if you put it round the rims of your pots. Another effective form of control is to put lots of grit around things like sweet peas and other vulnerable plants. You need to make sure that there is at least 5cm (2in) around the plants with no gaps for the snails to get through. It is an expensive way of controlling them but worth it on special plants.

You can also use beer traps: using a plastic bottle, cut off the end that you drink from, about a third of the way down the bottle, turn it round and put the drinking end into the bottle, then fill with cheap beer – that way once the slug is in the slug pub it can't escape. Using a torch after a rainfall at night is a good time to go out collecting, and sometimes it is a great incentive to children for earning a penny a snail! It can get quite competitive to see who gets the most snails.

You can buy organic slug pellets from hardware stores and the organic gardening catalogue. These are not harmful to pets, wildlife or humans and you only need four or five pellets around your plants. Like all slug pellets, they need reapplying after a period of time.

There is also a biological control available in the form of nematodes (microscopic worms), which are naturally present in the soil but you can buy them by mail order and then mix them with water and apply to the soil. You must make sure that the soil is at the correct temperature (see packet for instructions) for the nematodes to work. This is an excellent form of control but may be expensive for the allotment gardener if used on a large area. The nematodes get inside the slug and eat it from the inside out – not a very appealing end but as these nematodes are present in the soil anyway, but in smaller quantities, it seems preferable to slug pellets containing metaldehyde.

Aphids

Aphids, commonly known as greenfly, blackfly, etc., are one of the commonest garden pests. They may also be yellow, pink, grey or woolly. Some are winged and can travel long distances on the wind.

Woolly aphid on an apple tree.

There are over five hundred species in Great Britain, with various life cycles. They feed on the sap of plants by inserting sylets into the plant tissue and sucking out the sap from the cells; if not controlled they can cause severe damage. They also spread virus diseases from plant to plant.

They breed very prolifically, females giving birth to live young which mature in about a week and consequently one female could have millions of descendants in a season.

Symptoms of aphids include obvious infestation, particularly at the buds or tips of plants, curled and distorted leaves and honeydew and possibly associated sooty mould, which is a blackish fungal infection. You may find aphids on many different vegetables. Black bean aphid is the most serious of all broad bean pests as it stunts growth and damages the flowers, which in turn distorts the pods. They also attack many other plants including fruit; cherry foliage can be severely distorted by blackfly. They overwinter as eggs which hatch when the weather is warm enough around the end of March.

Methods of control include insectivorous birds such as tits, which you can encourage onto the allotment by feeding in winter and putting up nest boxes. Ladybirds and lacewings are also big aphid-eaters. They can be encouraged by avoiding insecticides, which would otherwise harm them; if you have aphids it is likely you will get ladybirds and lacewings. I generally blast aphids off with a powerful hose. I also make a mixture of a tablespoon of soap flakes dissolved in some hot water and one teaspoon of cooking oil in a plant spray bottle topped up with water. This can be sprayed on safely and save you money on products from the garden centre. Do not use washing-up liquid as it will burn the leaves. The oil helps the mixture to stick to the plant.

Whitefly tend to be a problem in glasshouses where they attack tomatoes and cucumbers. They

Aphid damage on runner beans.

enjoy the warm conditions that a glasshouse offers. Putting up sticky traps will help you to identify if you have whitefly and indeed many other pests. If whitefly is a problem you can use a biological control, which is very effective if used correctly. This comes in the form of a parasitic wasp called *Encarsia Formosa* and if conditions are right, e.g. there are plenty of whitefly for the *Encarsia* to eat and the temperature is right, it can be an excellent control measure.

Another form of whitefly is the cabbage whitefly, which is hardier and survives outside on brassicas. The females can lay up to 200 eggs, which hatch and pupate as scales before the adults emerge. They reproduce in 3–4 weeks. They are usually on the undersides of leaves and when you disturb the leaves they will fly off in a cloud. Because the whitefly is often on the undersides of leaves this is another good reason why spraying with chemicals is not a good idea; often the spray will not reach the affected part of the plant. Derris dust is an organic product and can be used outside to control the problem but this must be done frequently to be effective.

Red spider mite

Red spider mite are very small and not red at all! They attack a whole range of fruit, vegetables and ornamental plants. They are very small and difficult to see but mites develop colonies on the underside of leaves and spin a very fine web that is sometimes visible.

There is a biological control for the glasshouse mite called *Phytoselulus persimillis*, but it would not work outside as conditions are not right for it, so try derris if spider mite is a problem. You can spot spider mite damage as the leaves develop a yellowish mottling which turns bronze and the leaves may wither.

Caterpillars

Leaf-eating caterpillars are the larvae of moths and butterflies and there are many different species that are plant-specific in their attack. Others however are not so discriminating and munch their way through a range of plants. They attack annuals, perennials and also of course love vegetables. The green velvety angle-shades moth attacks dahlias, gladiolus and many other perennials. The cabbage white is a slightly hairy caterpillar and the females can lay several hundred eggs so there may be many generations within a season. These caterpillars skeletonize the leaves of brassicas and other annuals and perennials. The colourful and hairy vapourer moth is a pest of trees and shrubs. It is easy to spot the damage they cause and the best way to deal with them organically is to pick them off when you see the first sign of them or use fine netting.

Vine weevils

Vine weevils are the curse of the gardener because they can really devastate your plants and it is hard to protect your plants against attack. The adults are nearly all female and reproduce parthenogenically (they do not need a male partner). The bites that they take from the leaves do very little harm but it is upsetting because it shows that they are around and may have laid their eggs by the roots of your plants. Each weevil can lay hundreds of eggs. It is the grub stage of the vine weevil that is so destructive since they live off roots. These wrinkled white grubs are extremely destructive both outdoors and under glass. Some of their favourite targets are plants in containers. The effect on your plants will depend on the size of the root system and the number of grubs eating them. To start with the growth

Left: A glasshouse can provide a warm environment for pests to breed.

Below: Flea beetles tend to attack brassicas.

will slow down and the plant may then begin to wilt and then die as it no longer has enough roots to keep it alive.

Adult vine weevils cannot fly and they walk around at night so you can often see them; they are easy to destroy. You can also get a biological control in the form of nematodes that lay their eggs in the vine weevil grub, which then hatch to feed on the vine weevil. The nematodes come in powdered form and are watered on in late summer, while the soil is still warm (the soil temperature needs to be above 5°C in the daytime), but the grubs are, hopefully, still small enough not to have caused too much damage. If damage is a problem, it is possible to remove plants from their pots, squash the grubs and repot. There is also a compost available that contains nematodes that will deter these pests.

Flea beetle

It is important to mention the flea beetle as this is a real problem for the allotment-holder. It tends to be a pest of seedlings, especially attacking those in the cabbage family, which includes swedes, turnips and

radishes. They seem to be more of a serious problem during warm periods when it is also dry around April and May time. Small round holes appear in the leaves and the plant may grow very slowly. You can see the beetles as they jump when the plant is disturbed. To avoid them make sure you water well when the weather is dry and you can spray or dust with derris, which is organic, if you want to.

It is worth noting that derris is one of the strongest and longest lasting of the organic pest

Broad beans are subject to fungal problems.

controls. It also controls caterpillars, aphids, thrips and sawfly. The active ingredient is rotenone, which is derived from a number of tropical plants. You can use it up to one day before harvesting, but it is best used on dry days as it is not soluble in water.

DISEASES

Diseases are caused by fungi, bacteria or viruses and it is worth spending a bit of time reading about the difference between them.

- Fungi are related to plants but they do not photosynthesize (the process by which green plants and other organisms turn carbon dioxide and water into carbohydrates and oxygen, using light energy trapped by chlorophyll). Fungi obtain food from living or dead organic matter such as other plants. Some fungi are plant-specific and others attack many different plants. Examples of fungi are mildew and grey mould, rust and honey fungus.

- Bacteria are single-celled micro-organisms and they usually infect plants through wounds. An example would be canker.
- Viruses can infect many plants, including fruit, vegetables and ornamentals. The virus, like the common cold, infects the whole plant and this means that if plants are propagated by vegetative methods (not seed), for example bulbs and tubers, it is inevitably passed on to the next generation. Viruses are also carried by insects, and aphids and eelworms are common carriers. That is why when you buy your soft fruit is important to buy virus-free certified varieties. An example of a virus is potato leaf roll virus.

These are some of the diseases that the allotment-holder is likely to encounter.

Powdery mildew

This is a fungal disease that affects many plants. Again some of these are plant-specific and others are able to attack many different plants. This fungal

Potato blight – brown patches develop around the edges and tips of the leaves.

disease is spread by spores and they can be carried for long distances in the wind. Powdery mildew is worsened in warm, dry conditions. A white powdery mould appears on the leaves, stems and buds. Young growth is particularly affected. It looks unsightly and can cause leaves to drop early. If the plant is well established this is a relatively harmless disease. However, care should be taken with younger plants since these may be drastically weakened.

Remove all the dead leaves in autumn to prevent the spores from overwintering. Mulch the plants well in the spring and autumn with well-rotted manure to prevent the roots from drying out. If possible prune plants such as fruit bushes that are very prone to mildew to allow the air to move through the branches. This type of mildew affects apples, plums, peaches, peas, turnips, roses and fruit bushes.

Grey mould/botrytis

Grey or white mould is a very common problem because the fungus can be spread by rain, water splashes or on the air – it can also thrive on live or dead plant material and affects apples, strawberries, brassicas, lettuces, and dahlias to name but a few. It attacks buds and fruits and it can also affect stored fruits. Before the mould appears the leaves and stems often become discoloured. It thrives in damp conditions where plants are overcrowded. This is one of the reasons why spacing plants correctly is very important as it improves ventilation and air circulation. So consequently good hygiene will reduce the risk of this disease and keeping cutting tools clean will help as well. It spreads very quickly so cut back any infected plants and make sure all the plant debris is cleared away.

Potato blight

Potatoes and tomatoes are in the same family (*Solonaceae*), and so both tend to suffer from blight. The cause of the blight is a fungus called *Phytophthora infestans*. The spores are spread by the wind and rain, and the problem is particularly bad when humidity is high.

The first signs of blight appear in early summer as brown or black areas at the tips and margins of the leaves of both potatoes and tomatoes; they then curl and wither. This disease spreads very quickly and causes the plant to collapse. The spores can also spread from the leaves to the potatoes in the ground and then the tubers become infected with a firm reddish-brown rot under discoloured skin. When you are harvesting your potatoes and they come into contact with live spores the tubers will develop blight in store. They usually develop a secondary infection, which makes them smell terrible. To prevent this problem, make sure you earth up (pull earth up around the tubers in a mound using a hoe) the stems to keep the tubers covered. If you see any signs of infected leaves make sure you cut the leaves down immediately. It is also possible to buy blight-resistant varieties, such as 'Romano', 'Maris Piper' or 'Pentland Crown', if blight is a problem. Tomatoes show signs of blight by developing brown sunken areas and then rot. Of course, outdoor tomatoes are more susceptible due to weather conditions, and crop rotation is essential with all members of this family.

Try to consult with other allotment-holders to find out if this has been a problem in the past.

Rust

Rust is a very common problem on ornamental plants such as hollyhocks and roses, and it also attacks plants such as leeks and garlic. Onions are also sometimes affected. Rust is a very nasty fungus and this is a disease that tends to appear unnoticed and then erupts, especially in damp places, as orange-brown pustules that appear on the undersides of leaves. As always, good hygiene is essential and the adding of organic matter really helps as it opens up the soil and also adds nutrients. It's just common sense most of the time; like us, plants need good food, water and shelter from the elements and attacks from allotment enemies.

Other diseases

There are many other fungal diseases which can affect your plants; make sure you get hold of a good pest and disease book to help you identify them. Bordeaux mixture, which is a blend of copper sulphate and slaked lime dissolved to make a fungicidal spray, combats many fungal diseases such as blight on potatoes and tomatoes, raspberry cane spot and many other fungal infections.

I think it is worth mentioning cucumber mosaic virus as it is very common. Viruses are often carried by insects, so keeping your plants free from aphids etc. will help. Viruses can also be in the seed or pollen of a plant; always check with the grower that you have virus-free stock. There is no cure for the virus, but it is best to remove any infected plants and keep the plant free from pests. Do not use for propagation purposes. The symptoms tend to be a mottling or streaking of the leaves and sometimes there is a distortion of the foliage – it may curl up or look very crumpled. This is another good reason for buying certified stock when possible.

WEATHER DAMAGE

You may sometimes see the term disorder and this usually refers to frost, or wind damage, drought or waterlogging. Don't forget that frost damage usually occurs with the first frost of autumn or late spring frosts – another thing to make a note of in your diary so you are ready with your horticultural fleece to put over any tender plants. One of the main problems for the allotment-holder is the risk of the buds being killed on the fruit trees. Frost tends to roll downhill and that is why care should be taken when choosing your allotment site. This is also where a cold frame, cloche or polytunnel comes in handy, or of course you can use fleece, straw or bracken to cover vulnerable plants.

Wind can cause havoc on the allotment, so again

Rust is very common on alliums.

think about this when selecting your site. It can increase water loss, scorch the plants, and of course break off stems and branches. It will also put off pollinating insects from visiting your plants and this will lead to lack of fruit and vegetables later on.

Drought is another big problem, especially at this time of climate change, so make sure you water your plants at the most critical points in their life, for example, as the seedling, when transplanting and also when the plant is coming into fruit or flowering. Make sure you collect rainwater, dig in organic matter, mulch like mad and remove the weeds that will compete with your flowers and vegetables for moisture. Make sure you are aware of plants that need less water and do some trials for yourself to see how plants cope under stress.

Waterlogging is a problem for the gardener as it stops oxygen getting to the roots. Leaves may turn yellow and start to wilt and of course you may also see your roots beginning to rot. This is often a problem on heavy clay soils so again add more muck and also grit to individual plants if the structure of the soil needs it.

CHAPTER 9

Wildlife

One of the most exciting aspects of having an allotment is the ability to observe wildlife. Many allotments are situated in fantastic surroundings and a lot of these sites are visited by wildlife, some friendly and helpful – and some very unwelcome.

In this chapter we will look at ways to encourage some friendly visitors.

PONDS

Creating a pond is one of the best ways of attracting wildlife onto an allotment. A pond can be as simple as an old sink or bowl in your glass house or polytunnel. You can even use a children's paddling pool; this will not only attract wildlife such as frogs to deal with glasshouse pests, but will also raise the humidity in the glasshouse. However, to provide the best conditions for your wildlife a purpose-built pond is the best.

Building a pond is a great job for the winter, although it will establish more quickly if it is made in the springtime. Before you start, think carefully about where the pond is to be sited as it will be a permanent feature in your allotment. Choose a sunny sheltered spot that receives some shade throughout the day, but make sure you avoid overhanging trees. This is because autumn leaves in a pond can create problems with pests and diseases. Try to choose a level area on your allotment; it is possible to make a pond on a gentle slope if you make one bank deeper.

As a note of caution, do think twice about a pond if you have small children. If there are children around, consider putting a fence round the pond,

A wildlife 'hotel' makes an attractive feature.

as children can drown in just a very small amount of water.

Making your pond

To prepare your pond, mark out the shape using some string or a piece of hosepipe. You could also use some dry sand poured from a bottle to mark your outline. Try to get an irregular rounded shape so that the pond looks more natural; this will provide more mini-habitats with a variety of depth and temperature. When you feel happy with the shape, remove any weeds and grass, but save some of them to create a bank behind the pond. This will make another interesting feature. Make sure that the sides of the pond are gently sloping as this will allow pond creatures a way out, and also make sure they are wide enough for planting marginal plants; these are plants that like to have their feet wet all the time, and consequently need a shelf to sit on that is about 20cm (8in) deep. One area of the pond should be at least 70–100cm (2–3ft) deep; if your pond is large it will need to be even deeper, so that it provides protection for animals in extremes of heat and cold. The last thing to do is to make sure there are no stones or other sharp objects that will tear the pond liner.

At this stage you can then put either old carpet down or some sand. If neither of these are available, you can use cardboard, sacking or even newspaper – anything that will act as a barrier between the liner and the soil and will help to protect the liner from stones, etc.

Next calculate how much liner you will need. The best way to do this is to measure the maximum length and width of the pond, then add on twice the depth to each dimension. So for example if a pond

Left: A pond under construction…

Below: … and six months later. Note the willow tunnel for children.

Plants will help to keep your pond free of algae.

is 4m in length, 3m in width and 0.5m deep, the size of the liner will be 4m + 1m by 3m + 1m, i.e. 5m by 4m – in other words, 20sq m. There are a range of liners available and if you want your pond to last you will need to buy that one that is UV-resistant and will last at least twenty years; it will also need to stretch. It will be quite expensive so check out the prices before you start. Buying off the internet from a pond supplier is probably your best bet.

Having got your liner, roll it over the pond, ensuring that there is a good overlap on all sides of at least 30cm, and then trim any excess away. Put a layer of sand or subsoil in the bottom of the pond; this will hide the liner and provide a place for pond creatures to hide and also a growing medium for plants.

Now for the exciting part; let the water trickle in gently so that it doesn't disturb the soil in the bottom. While it is filling up, you can put either turf or stones around the edge of the pond. It is best to leave the pond for a week or so before planting it up.

Oxygenating your pond

Your pond will need some oxygenators – submerged plants that will help to keep the water clear by competing with algae for minerals and carbon dioxide. You could try either hornwort (*Ceratophyllum demersum*) or milifoil (*Myriophyllum spicatum*), both of which can be kept under control as some oxygenators are very invasive. For your marginal shelf you could try marsh marigold (*Caltha palustris*) or water iris (*Iris laevigata*).

To keep the water clear, you will need to cover about fifty per cent of the surface with plant leaves so look out for some deep-water plants as well, such as water lilies (*Nymphoides* species). Other plants can be used to float in the water and do not need soil; these include frogbit (*Hydrocharis morsus ranea*), which is lovely with its white flowers, or the water chestnut (*Trapa natans*); although this is an annual plant it can propagate itself from seed that overwinters in the bottom of the pond.

Bog gardens
You could also make a bog garden at the end of the pond, making sure you use the end that slopes to 'catch' the water. Use a piece of the left-over liner to line the bog garden and make holes in it at regular intervals so that the excess water can drain away. If you manage to create a really good boggy area then you could try and grow some prickly rhubarb (*Gunnera manicata*). This is a magnificent plant with amazing rhubarb-like leaves that can grow up to 2m (6ft) across. However, it must have moisture to thrive.

To find out more, go to a good website such as the RHS or get a book on pond plants; you will see that it is another whole world of plants! Moreover, as well as water attracting a wide range of wildlife, a pond really is lovely to sit by in the summer.

Visitors to your pond

Make sure that the edges of the pond are well planted to provide homes for pond life. Ornamental grasses such as *Miscanthus* varieties and *Calamagrostis* look great around a pond and grow tall after a couple of seasons. Another good grass to grow is *Arundo donax*. Although this dies back in

Native shrubs will attract a variety of friendly wildlife.

the winter, it grows very tall in one season. The other advantage of having grasses around the pond is that they provide food for the birds over winter. Cut the deciduous grasses down in the spring and take out the dead stems of the evergreen ones.

Your pond will attract frogs, toads, dragonflies and damselflies, newts and water boatmen, pond skaters and many other visitors. If you have adolescent children, hopefully your pond will also attract them! My children, when going through the gardening-is-boring stage, always wanted to come and look at the magical happenings in a pond, whether the fascination of mating frogs in the spring or just watching the pond teeming with life. It is amazing how quickly the wildlife arrives when you have made a pond. Many wildlife websites have identification sheets so that you can tell the difference between the pond insects.

ENCOURAGING FRIENDLY WILDLIFE

The more variety there is within the structure and design of your allotment garden, the greater the number of options there are for wildlife to visit or

SEED PLANTS FOR WILDLIFE

- Angelica (*Angelica sylvestris*)
- Clematis (*Clematis spp*)
- Globe thistle (*Echinops ritro*)
- Golden rod (*Solidago candensis*)
- Greater knapweed (*Centaura scabios*)
- Honesty (*Lunaria annua*)
- Meadowsweet (*Filipendual ulmaria*)
- Sunflower (*Helianthus annus*)
- Teasel (*Dipsacus sylvestris*)
- Yarrow (*Achillea spp*)

Buddleia attracts butterflies – this picture shows a comma enjoying the nectar.

reside there. For example, consider different heights of hard landscaping, pergolas, sheds, etc, as well as the plants. Also, if you curve your borders then you are more likely to increase the number of aspects to the sun. On your allotment, try to create 'safe' corridors for animals and insects to move along without being seen.

Try to include some small trees as some birds like to sing from a high 'song post'. Native trees will support a huge number of insects. For example, oak (*Quercus*) supports 284 species of birds and insects, willow (*Salix*) 266, birch (*Betula*) 229 and hawthorn (*Crataegus*) 149. In contrast, the non-native plants such as sweet chestnut and rhododendron support respectively just three and one insect species. Most animals are dependent on specific local plants; they have unique haunts and habitats and reproduce only when conditions are right. For instance, the caterpillar of the small tortoiseshell butterfly will eat only stinging nettles; without honeysuckle we would not have the white admiral butterfly; and goldfinches need seeds. If we use native

This Rosa rugosa *makes a good hedge, as well as providing large hips for winter interest and wildlife.*

A welcome home for insects can be easily constructed.

plants on our allotments, this has the benefit of assisting with the food chain. (Although we welcome birds and butterflies, we must also try to live with the so-called pests such as caterpillars – as of course caterpillars turn into butterflies!) When you are out and about look out for the plants that seem to be literally buzzing and make a note of them.

Hedges are a must for the allotment and one that contains a variety of species is best for wildlife; one with a large number of native plants is even better. Try to use honeysuckle (*Lonicera*) and wild roses (*Rosa canina*). The dark purple sloes of the black-thorn (*Prunus spinosa*) make a great specimen for exposed allotments, while holly (*Ilex aquifolium*) and ivy (*Hedera helix*) supply berries for birds through the winter and cheer up the allotment, providing foliage to pick at Christmastime.

Some simple hints for encouraging wildlife

Try to leave a small area of grass to grow long as this provides a good home for spiders, moths, grasshoppers and beetles. You could add some wildflowers to give some interest. It is best to grow wildflowers in plugs rather than scattering seed as the grass will just out-compete the flowers. Look around your local area to see which wild flowers grow well there. Grow a mixture of native and non-native plants to provide nectar and pollen for the bees and other insects. Use the internet to find out which flowers are native to your area.

Try to leave seed heads on plants over the winter; they will perform two functions, providing food for the birds and insects and also a home for some insects to live in. They also look wonderful with a hoar frost on them!

Another way to encourage wildlife to your allotment is to plant climbers up against your sheds or fences to provide cover. Don't forget that wrens and robins like to nest low so put a couple of old kettles in your climbers and you never know, you may find a family of birds living there.

The compost heap not only provides food for your garden, but it is also a place for animals and invertebrates to live. Slow worms love the damp and warmth of the compost heap and will often appear and wink at you when you turn over the compost. Many of the other species such as beetles and birds find food there.

Next time you go to throw out an old feather-filled pillow, remove the feathers and put them in an old hanging basket, so the birds can use them to build their nests. Human hair is also a help to the birds when they are building nests, so next time you have your hair cut keep the clippings and put them where the birds can use them.

A log pile is often suggested for encouraging wildlife. Try using two or three old pallets piled on top of one another. Use bamboo canes, twigs, engineering bricks with holes in them, straw, pine cones, teasels and any other attractive organic material to gradually fill up your wildlife condominium. Drill holes in logs and this will make a home for beetles, mining bees and other insects. To make your condominium complete turf the roof and grow wild flower plugs in it. Dead wood is

Above: This bee seems to be attracted by the colour of Bracteantha bracteata.

Right: Lunaria annua *(Honesty) seed pods provide food for birds and look good well into winter.*

Euonymous europaeus (spindle) berries are stunningly good looking and wonderful food for the birds.

really important for a huge range of invertebrates, many of which, including the fantastic stag beetle, suffer from lack of habitat in the wild. Log piles are best sited in cool, damp shady spots. There are many beetle species that lay their eggs in logs under the soil, and after hatching, the larvae chew their way through the decaying wood. Hedgehogs and toads may hibernate in large piles of wood, while blackbirds and chaffinches that nest close to the ground may find a home to bring up their family.

Animal-friendly plants

By planting flowers that contain a high quantity of pollen and nectar you can encourage bees, butterflies and hoverflies into your garden. Borage (*Borago officinalis*) is a great plant for encouraging bees, while planting sweetpeas amongst your runner beans will encourage pollinators. Basically flowers that look attractive are not there for our benefit – they are there to attract pollinating insects. Pale colours, in particular pinks and mauves, are often more attractive to bees and butterflies than very bright colours. The shape of the flower is also very important, for example the poached egg plant (*Limnanthus douglasii*) has a very open flower, as do hellebores and hardy geraniums; these provide a landing pad for insects and the arrangement of their open flowers makes it easy for the insects to access the pollen. Some plants like Buddleia, Echinacea and *Verbena bonariensis* are designed to hold lots of nectar; this is so that butterflies can dip their tongues into the plant to feed easily. Plants with bell-shaped flowers, such as campanulas and foxgloves, have honey guides that act as landing lights to guide the insects in.

Plants such as honeysuckle (*Lonicera*) and night-scented stock, as well as *Mahonia* and *Nicotiana*, all smell their best at night and are pollinated by moths, which in turn are the food for bats.

Try to plant things that will have long flowering periods and don't forget that very showy bedding plants tend not to have much benefit for wildlife; neither do double-flowered plants because the insects can't find their way in. A lot of the old cottage garden plants are ideal. If possible, avoid planting your insect-friendly plants in cold windy parts of the allotment as they will not have many visitors. It will be easier for insects to find food if there is a group of plants so that the colour and scent is highly visible and the perfume is strong.

Plant these high nectar and pollen plants in with your vegetables to ensure good pollination. Herbs are also good for attracting insects, and the majority

BERRY-PRODUCING PLANTS

- Barberry (*Berberis spp*)
- Bramble (*Rubus spp*)
- Elderberry (*Sambucus nigra*)
- Guelder rose (*Viburnum opulus*)
- Holly (*Ilex aquifolium*)
- Japanese quince (*Chaenomeles spp*)
- Oregon grape (*Mahonia spp*)
- Pyracantha (*Pyracantha spp*)
- Spindle (*Euonymus europaeus*)
- Yew (*Taxus baccata*)

of them are drought-resistant. One of the most critical times of year for wildlife is from autumn to early spring, so plants that produce plenty of fruits and seeds have good value.

CHAPTER 10

Involving children

Like many things we do, allotment gardening often reflects a phase in our lives; not for everyone, of course, as there are many people who have allotments for years. One of the reasons for this is often that when children reach a certain age it is difficult to take them to the allotment as there is nothing to hold their interest. However, gardening in schools is something that seems to be coming back in style, and hopefully will become a fashionable pursuit for children and young people.

If you have children or are planning to have children, it is important when choosing your allotment to take time to think about the practicalities of getting children there; for example, is it a long walk from the gate, is there any shelter, etc. If you begin by making your space child-friendly then it will certainly pay dividends eventually.

One of the obvious ways is to share your allotment with other families. In this way you won't feel so much responsibility for your allotment and at the same time you can share tasks such as watering, digging and planting. Make sure you set ground rules in the beginning and decide who is to be responsible for what.

YOUNG CHILDREN

It often seems easier to entertain younger children as there are some obvious attractions for them. A sandpit is always fun, but make sure you put a cover over it when not in use to stop animals using it as a loo! If possible, try to find some seat-sized tree stumps to put around the sandpit so children can sit as well as play in the sand. You can use old tyres

A scarecrow might see off a few birds, but is also fun for children to make.

Children will enjoy making homemade bird feeders.

to make your sandpit; try to find the largest one available and paint it with a multisurface spray paint before filling it with sand. Just add a few scoops, buckets and spoons and it will provide hours of amusement for younger children.

A tepee or tent is another good way of keeping them amused, giving the sense of a place of their own in which to hide away from adults. It is easy to make your own using fabric attached to some canes in a wigwam shape. This can be taken down at the end of the day and stored away until next time.

There is a stage in every child's life when they

A play area will be an added attraction for children at the allotment.

become obsessed with poo! There are identification books and charts that are available and young children will have great fun identifying footprints in mud, droppings, movement patterns, and habitats of different species of birds and animals. Make sure you have a magnifying glass to hand.

For very young children keep a box of shells, pebbles, cones and crystals for them to play with; young children love sorting and examining such things. Have a blackboard nearby – you can write a what-to-do list on it and the children can use it to draw on.

A swing and slide is something that you can often pick up secondhand and it is worth getting one if your children are small – they will play on it until they are at least seven or eight. You can of course make your own and one way of doing it is to construct a frame and grow runner beans over it – giving a real sense of privacy; it looks wonderful too. You can use old railway sleepers cemented into the ground at an angle and then sling a hammock between the sleepers. This may even entice your teenager to visit, if only for a rest. Use reed or bamboo screening to create a secluded area.

Rope ladders are good fun but need a frame to attach to. If you are really ambitious, you could make a climbing frame or buy one secondhand – these are often for sale on the internet or in local papers.

Water plays a very important part in young children's lives so make sure you have plenty of watering cans and other receptacles available for them to play with. A paddling pool for hot summer days is a must – try to find one that has sides that are already constructed, that way you don't have to spend hours blowing it up.

Involve children in making a scarecrow; they will really love finding old clothes to dress the scarecrow in. Use a pillow case to draw the face on, then stuff your scarecrow with old plastic bags; this will stop your scarecrow from getting damaged too quickly in the wet. Broom handles or hazel poles make a suitable frame, but remember to site your scarecrow away from the wind as your allotment guest may blow over and become damaged.

OLDER CHILDREN

Something else to consider is older children, and how you will persuade them to at least visit your allotment. For older children a project may help to hold their attention whilst you are planting out your seedlings. For example you could give them an old chair or table that is past its best and some old crockery, then let them use mosaic to decorate it. They will have to draw a simple design before putting on the tiles. Make sure you use swimming pool cement and grout so that it is weatherproof.

Ensure you have plenty of paint and brushes at your allotment – not just for you but also for children. Visit your local fruit and vegetable market where you will find all sorts of different wooden boxes. Take them to your allotment and encourage children to paint them; they then make really good planters that can be decorated. Stand the boxes on

Children are pleased to be involved and making mosaic paving stones can be very creative.

upturned flower pots to give some drainage, line them with a bin bag and make some holes in the bottom for drainage, before filling them with soil.

Providing older children with lots of hazel poles and other pieces of logs and wood will hopefully give them the incentive to build a den. Hazel is a good wood to start off the structure with and then it can gradually be built up over time to make a hideaway. Use autumn leaves or even a camouflage net to keep it a 'secret' place.

Source some willow and plant it up to make a living willow arbour, tunnel or seat; the children can tie in the willow when it has grown, which is a very satisfying task. All you need to do is to push the willow into the ground and it will grow. If your soil is poor, add some organic matter as willow needs a moisture-retentive soil. Remember to water it and it will soon take off and grow into a living willow structure.

If you can find some unwanted decking, make a seating area with it and put it in a shady place, making another place to sit – add some cushions and children can enjoy the space. Have a box of board games at the ready for children to play when they get bored.

SOWING AND GROWING

Try to create special areas for the children to garden for themselves. Scaffold boards are brilliant for this purpose. Just screw four scaffolding boards together in a square and let the children paint them. Put topsoil and garden compost in them and an obelisk in the middle to grow runner beans up.

A willow arbour can easily be constructed.

Giving children their own part of the allotment can also be useful as they can then design and choose what they want to grow. Salad crops are always good, as are herbs and hardy annuals. Pumpkins are a must for late summer and tomatoes and anything that is quick-growing is good.

Seed-sowing appeals to most people and of course sunflowers are a must for young children. Try encouraging them to plant pips from fruit they have eaten as well – this will give them a sense of life cycles. Salad crops are also a good choice for growing from seed as they mature very quickly. If you want to interest teenagers, get them involved in the cooking part as well – cooking is very 'in' at present, so grab the moment!

Strawberries are another plant that will give a lot of pleasure to children. Alpine strawberries are prolific fruiters and they can be grown as edging and look and taste fantastic. Try growing strawberries from seed; start them off at home and then tempt your children to come and plant them at the allotment!

Even if children are not around when you plant your potatoes, harvesting them is certainly a lovely allotment task. Just the warmth of the soil when you dig them up is a pleasure and pulling up your buried treasures is always a treat.

This 'Teddy bear' variety of sunflower is easy to grow and the results are delightful.

ALLOTMENT ACTIVITIES

- Collecting seeds and packaging them up is a great way of saving money – something that always appeals to teenagers.
- Designing packets as well may encourage them to come to the allotment and do some sketching.
- My children enjoy photographing plants, and turning them into cards, etc. Trying to capture plants and wildlife is good fun.
- Groups of children and young people like making things together and making mobiles is an enjoyable activity. Supply lots of sticks, shells, beads, cones and large seeds for them to thread and then they can hang them around the allotment.
- Making a compost heap and keeping a wormery may appeal to slightly older children.
- Various gardening suppliers sell games for playing outside – connect four, jenga, chess, etc, are all possibilities.

- Make a hopscotch area using old floor tiles.
- Make a mosaic hopscotch area. Construct a wooden frame by nailing four pieces of wood together. Put the frame on a polythene sheet and almost fill it with cement. Use some black pebbles to lay out the numbers in the frame, and then fill in the background with some white pebbles to give a mosaic effect, pushing them well in. Leave for a week before using it to allow the cement to reach its full strength.
- Let the children plant up their old shoes, making sure you make some holes in between the stitching of the sole for drainage.
- Use some of the herbs that you have grown to make herbal teas – mint and lemon balm make a delicious tea and borage flowers can be picked and frozen in ice cube trays to add to drinks.
- Compact discs are great for keeping the birds off your vegetables, as they project flashes of light and also move when the breeze catches them. Involve children in decorating them – a lovely job for a winter's day.

Above: Painting CDs and suspending them above crops really does deter pests.
Left: Old wellies make good containers.

These strawberries may not make it home!

Older children may enjoy the scientific aspect of gardening, for example soil-testing, propagation, plant life cycles, seed germination, etc. Plant naming and which family a plant belongs to may also interest young people and may fit in with school studies. The way a compost heap works and how soil is made, together with introducing them to 'good' and 'bad' insects, as well as looking at plant adaptations, for example cacti and succulents, plants for shade, etc. are also fascinating subjects for children. Introduce them to plants that will attract wildlife and try to make a nectar bar in a sunny spot on the allotment so they can watch bees and butterflies at work.

ANIMAL MAGIC

Wildlife is always a good crowd-puller with children, and most of them love watching frogs, toads and slow worms, all of which are rather magical. Chapter 9 has plenty of suggestions for attracting wildlife to your allotment. Encourage children to research in books and on the internet about the fascinating lifecycles of native wildlife.

Making a lacewing hotel is a good project for children on your allotment. All you need is a plastic bottle and some corrugated card. Cut the bottom off the bottle, roll up the corrugated card and put it

Make a nectar bar using Phacelia, *which is a green manure and quick to germinate.*

in the bottle. Make two small holes opposite each other at the bottom of the bottle, then thread a piece of wire through them to stop the card falling out. Twist another piece of wire around the bottle top and hang it on a tree or a bush. It is best to leave the top on the bottle so that rain cannot get in and make it soggy.

Another good idea for attracting wildlife is to take some hollow stems from plants such as bamboo, *Kerria* or *Leycesteria*, and tie them together, then place them in the hedge or in the trees. Hopefully they will be visited by mining bees. These are solitary bees, which will lay their eggs inside the stems, which in turn will help them to perform their vital role of pollinating your flowers, fruit and vegetables.

SEASONAL ACTIVITIES

One of the joys of allotment gardening is watching the passing of the seasons. Children can be encouraged to appreciate seasonal change by introducing different activities according to the time of year.

Spring

In early spring, tie some pieces of cotton in trees and shrubs and allow the birds to take this for nest-building. You could also put up a hanging basket full of feathers from an old pillow to help the birds with nest-building.

One later spring attraction for the children is to provide an Easter egg hunt; this will keep them busy searching for hidden chocolate while you do a bit of weeding.

Make sure to involve them in sowing seeds and germination.

Summer

You could have an allotment party in the summer. Get the children involved in the preparations and planning and provide games and activities for them, including a treasure hunt and maybe a few races and a quiz that requires them to bring you leaves from certain trees, shrubs, etc, for a few prizes. Make a canopy where they can cool off and eat their picnic in the shade. Try to involve them in picking fruit, vegetables and herbs to make the food for the party.

THREE SISTERS GARDENING

Three sisters gardening is a North American Indian idea that may well appeal to older children. It involves producing three crops that young people can pick and eat, The crops support each other's growth and use only a relatively small amount of space.

Beans growing up sweet corn, as part of the three sisters method of gardening.

You will need an area about 2.0m (6ft) long and 1.5m (5ft) in width. Grow pumpkins on the ground and then sweetcorn inbetween the pumpkins, and pole beans to climb up the corn, using the corn as a support. All these things can be started off under glass and planted out in May when danger of frost has passed.

Autumn

A good end-of-summer activity is to plant a daffodil maze. Let the children design it by laying out two old hose pipes or string in a spiral design. Arrange the bulbs in a single layer in the spiral, in between the ropes, then plant them to about twice the depth of the bulbs. Continue round the maze. These will look wonderful in the spring and will come up every year. After flowering, you will need to leave the leaves of the daffodils for six weeks before mowing so they can build up energy for next year's flowers. You could alternatively do the same in May using sweetcorn.

Painting signs is a good distraction in the winter months.

Hallowe'en is another time for celebration; besides all the excitement of dressing up, it is another excuse to get children to come to the allotment. There is such a lot to keep them occupied at this time, including carving pumpkins, hopefully ones they have grown themselves. Use grasses such as the black grass, *Ophiopogon planioscapus* 'Nigrescens', and *Carex* 'Frosted Curls' to make hair for the pumpkins.

This is also a good time to put up some bat boxes, and these may well attract even the most unwilling of allotmenteers. If you are having a children's Hallowe'en party at your allotment, this could add to the eerie glow of the pumpkin lanterns if you were able to entice a few bats as well! Hang up a white sheet and shine a torch on it – this will attract some moths along to the party as well. Have a few flares burning to add to the gothic feel, making sure you have a bucket of water nearby in case

of any accident. Use jam jars covered in tissue paper with eyes and mouths cut out to create glowing lanterns. Stick the tissue paper onto the jars using PVA glue, put string around the top and hang them around the allotment. Placing tea lights inside will give an attractive glow.

Autumn may be a good time to make a fire pit at your allotment, which is possibly something else that will attract older children, but check first that it will be allowed. Mark out the circle for the pit with a piece of string tied to a cane, by putting the cane into the earth where you intend the fire pit to be, then using some spray marker paint held at the end of the string to mark out the circle on the ground. Dig out a hole to the depth of 500mm (20in). If you want your fire pit to be permanent, add a few courses of engineering bricks to create an edge.

Make sure that you provide an escape ramp for small animals and that the fire pit is covered when unattended. Having a fire pit will given endless opportunities to attract people of all ages to your allotment.

As an alternative, look in scrap-metal merchants and see if you can find any interesting wrought-iron left-overs, which could be used to make a simple brazier to contain any fires.

Winter

Christmas is always a good time to get young people to at least go for one walk – take them to your allotment and make sure you have plenty to entertain them once they are there. For example, you could make a wreath using shining wrapped sweets rather than holly; just fasten the sweets together using florist's wire, bent into hairpin shapes and add to a polystyrene ring.

After Christmas is past, take your Christmas tree to the allotment and dress it for the birds. You can hang all sorts of things on it and it is great to watch the birds enjoy Christmas too! Tie fat-balls, peanuts threaded onto string, windfall apples, berries in clusters, fir cones and coconut shells filled with fat for them to feast on. Use brightly coloured ribbons to tie them onto the tree for a really festive effect.

Seeds are also a must for the birds' diet. You might be able to engage your teenagers in making a bird table.

SAFETY ISSUES

While your children are bound to suffer the usual minor cuts and bruises that are part of growing up, make sure that you check all the things you make with them, and teach them from an early age about such things as poisonous plants, sunburn, the dangers of water and all the other potential hazards that there are at the allotment. It is important not to quash their enthusiasm, but at the same time they need to be aware of the possible dangers. Just make sure you take as many reasonable steps as possible to ensure that your allotment is a safe place for your own and other people's children to be creative and play.

JOBS

- Transplant Nasturtium around apple trees
- Polytunnel door repair
- Plant out Melo

CHAPTER 11

Conclusion

PLANNING AHEAD

The wonderful thing about gardening is that it is very forgiving. If you didn't get round to things this year, then there is always next year when you can finish off or even start those projects that you were meaning to do. Even the most experienced gardeners forget to plant certain things at the correct time of year.

Keeping a diary as a reference is a must for the allotment gardener.

This will remind you what you need to do next year and point out mistakes that you made, things that went well and other projects to try.

Make sections for each month of the year, putting your seeds in order as to when they need to be sown. Make a note of any frustrations that you had during the previous season – string getting tangled, not being able to find secateurs, blunt blades on tools and mowers, etc – and make sure you put them right before you next go to the allotment. Decide which crops you will grow again and which ones didn't do so well.

Work out your crop rotation plan and make sure you make a note of how it will be set out.

Spend some time researching things that you need, such as hazel poles, netting, willow, scaffold boards, manure, and plan how you will get them to your allotment. Think about getting a polytunnel or greenhouse to protect your crops.

Make a list of jobs to be done.

MAINTAINING INTEREST

Take time to go and look at other allotments. Join the Royal Horticultural Society, as this will enable you to keep up with what is going on in the gardening world, introduce you to new plants and cultivars and also new methods of gardening in our changing climate. Look into joining your local horticultural society or allotment society. It is always helpful to be inspired by other gardeners and swap ideas.

If you found your allotment too much this year, think about sharing it or leaving one half covered with black polythene and mulch while you sort out the other half.

The best advice is to stay on top of your allotment tasks and you will enjoy your allotment year – there is nothing better than being part of the changing seasons and enjoying the fruits of your labours.

ALLOTMENT SOCIETIES

If there isn't one already, consider starting up an allotment society. It can be very straightforward – just arrange an annual get-together to sort out a bulk seed order. Or you can set up a more complex society that manages the allotment site with your local council's agreement. This would involve liaising with the council over leasing the site, as well as managing plot occupation and rent collection. The society can also take responsibility for capital expenditure on water, machinery, and so on. Local councils are often keen to encourage sites to self-manage and may be able to help you source funding and information. This scheme obviously demands more from its members, especially a committee, but it can be empowering and rewarding as

Decide which crops you will grow again and which did not do so well.

Choosing seeds well in advance can be fun.

the resulting allotment site is usually more lively, as it can involve the local community with events such as open days.

Some allotment societies work in partnership with the site owner. For example, the parish council might collect the rent and maintain the site, while the society might organize the shop, the annual plant sale and other events. This is a good arrangement as the council will deal with the administration, leaving the association free to concentrate on other services and events.

If you are a member of an allotment society or gardening club, you should be able to get a good discount on bulk orders of seed. For example

Thompson and Morgan gives societies and allotment-holders a fifty per cent discount on all seed orders, however small. The Kings Seeds allotment scheme offers fifty per cent off seed orders over £150 and a thirty-five per cent discount on orders of £150 and under. You will need to request a special catalogue for this scheme. The discount at Suttons Seeds ranges from ten to fifty-two per cent, depending on the size of the order. Franchi Seeds of Italy offers forty per cent off when you spend over £100. Marshalls gives twenty-five per cent off any order over £200 and the *Organic Gardening Catalogue* offers up to thirty per cent off group orders.

A calendar of allotment gardening tasks

DECEMBER AND JANUARY

The winter months are a good time to catch up with jobs that you haven't had time to finish earlier in the year and also to prepare for next spring. Now is the time to order seeds and seed potatoes, tidy up the shed and paint it, clean the greenhouse, collect plastic bottles to make mini-cloches, clean out your pots, and make sure the glass is repaired in cold frames. Take time to plan your crop rotation system for next year. Repair fences and make new compost bins, and collect as many receptacles as possible to use for water butts.

Start cleaning up pots in preparation for planting.

Vegetables

Sow indoors
Lettuces, radishes, round varieties of carrots, spinach, salad onions and turnips. Place them on the windowsill or in a propagator.

Winter on the allotment.

Clean cold frames and make sure glass is repaired ready for seedlings.

Plant outdoors
Garlic cloves, e.g. 'Thermidrome' and 'Printantor'.

Harvest
Jerusalem artichokes, perpetual spinach, Brussels sprouts, winter cabbage, savoy cabbage, carrots, celeriac, celery, chicory (non-forcing and forcing varieties), endive, kale, kohlrabi, leeks, lettuce, parsnip, radish, salsify, scorzonera, spinach, swede, turnips.

Fruit

- Plant rhubarb crowns.
- Cover established rhubarb to force early shoots.
- Cut down canes of autumn-fruiting raspberries that have finished fruiting and burn to prevent fungal diseases spreading.
- Plant bar-rooted fruit trees and bushes.
- Check that young trees are supported with stakes and ties.
- Winter prune young apples and pear trees.
- Place grease bands around tree trunks to

Rhubarb pushing up through the snow.

prevent winter moths from climbing trees and laying eggs.

Flowers

- Enjoy picking flowers and stems from the allotment.
- If you are growing *Helleborus niger* (Christmas rose), cover it with a cloche and it might flower at Christmas. Cut off old leaves of *Heleborus orientalis*.
- Sow seeds of hardy plants that need a chill before they can germinate. If you have collected seeds of trees, conifers or shrubs, they will need a cold spell. Put them in a pot of compost, cover them with grit, label and put them in a cold frame or quiet corner of the allotment. Keep watered during the winter.
- Deadhead winter pansies.
- Order seeds from catalogues.
- Check watering of any containers, bulbs or biennials if the weather is dry.

General tasks

- Continue digging over the ground and adding manure.
- Clean, oil and repair garden tools.
- Collect fallen leaves and store. Leaves break down to form leaf mould, which is an excellent soil conditioner.
- Collect remains of left-over vegetation and add to the compost heap.
- Feed the birds.
- Protect container plants with wrappings of straw or bubble-wrap to stop the root ball from freezing.

- Cover your compost bins to keep the rain out and the heat in.
- Set up extra water butts to collect rainwater from your greenhouse or shed roof. If you don't have a shed or greenhouse, set up a shelter with four posts and a sloping corrugated plastic roof; you can then attach guttering, a down pipe and a water butt.
- Make sure to check on your crops, and remove any that are diseased or rotten. Use carrying trays for pots to store apples and pears and anything else that will fit into each compartment. This will stop them touching each other and prevent disease.
- Remove the yellowing leaves from winter brassicas.
- Don't forget that if ponds freeze over, frogs can be deprived of oxygen, so float a small ball in the pond; this will allow a small area to be kept clear.
- Net winter vegetables to protect them from pigeons.
- Earth up any tall vegetables to prevent them from suffering wind damage.
- Clean out the bottoms of hedges.
- Test your soil for acidity and correct it by adding lime if necessary.
- Keep on top of weeds like groundsel and chickweed, which continue seeding over winter.

FEBRUARY

Winter is almost over.

Vegetables

The following sowing and planting times are for the south of England. If you live in the north, delay these for two to four weeks, depending on the weather. If there is a hard frost forecast, make sure you have some horticultural fleece handy to protect your germinating seeds. Order seeds, plan and clear the vegetable garden if you haven't already done so. Use cloches and cold frames for your early sowings to give them some protection.

Sow outdoors

Broad beans, parsnips, onions (from seed), peas for May/June crop (suitable varieties are 'Feltham First' and 'Meteor').

Sow under cover

Summer cabbage (e.g. varieties 'Greyhound', 'Hispi', 'Primo', 'Derby Day', 'Stonehead', 'Minicole', 'Winnigstadt'), radish (summer varieties), lettuce, rocket, spinach, early turnip, e.g. purple top Milan.

Sow under heated cover

Aubergine and pepper (for a greenhouse crop).

Plant outdoors

Jerusalem artichoke tubers and shallots.

Preparation

Start chitting early potato varieties in preparation for planting in later March/early April. Individual tubers can be placed in egg boxes in a cool place in indirect light.

Harvest

Jerusalem artichoke, perpetual spinach (leaf beet), early purple sprouting broccoli, Brussels sprouts, celeriac, celery, chicory, endive, kale, leeks, parsnip, radish, salsify, scorzonera, spinach, swede, turnip.

Fruit

- Check for canker on apples and pears.
- Check stakes and ties.
- If you have a wood burner, apply the ash to the bottom of fruit bushes, avoiding the stems. This will help with winter hardiness and fruiting.
- Plant new trees, bushes and vines.
- Cover your strawberries with polytunnels until March for an early crop.
- Take hardwood cuttings of blackcurrant bushes.
- Finish planting fruit trees and bushes; also raspberries and other cane fruits.
- Finish pruning apples and pears.
- Shorten sideshoots on red and white currants to just one bud and remove old stems crowding the centre of the bush.
- Prune gooseberries.
- Protect blooms on early flowering fruit trees – peaches, nectarines, apricots. You can use horticultural fleece attached to a frame and stand it against the tree.
- If you want early rhubarb, force a few crowns

by covering them with buckets or large plastic flower pots. Put a brick over the drainage hole to block out the light and to prevent the pot from blowing away. It is a good idea to place straw or compost over the buckets for added heat.

Plant dormant dahlia tubers for a good display later in the year.

Flowers

- Plant up a couple of containers with polyanthus and some spring bulbs. It will encourage you to visit your allotment if there is some colour to look at!
- Plant lily-of-the-valley crowns in dappled shady areas.
- Sow sweet peas under cover.
- Plant stored dahlia tubers in pots or boxes filled with potting compost in a frost-free greenhouse to get them off to an early start.

An unusual way to display spring bulbs.

- Pot up lily bulbs into pots in threes or fives half-way down and stand in a frost-free greenhouse.

General tasks
- Remove any volunteer potatoes to keep your plot free from blight.
- Prune hedges towards the end of the month if they are overgrown.
- Cut back newly-planted raspberry canes if they were not pruned when you planted them.
- Harvest green manure crops when the soil is ready to dig. Young lush growth can be chopped up and dug into the soil a few weeks before planting. More mature crops should be composted. Soil can be warmed up by covering it with plastic sheeting or with cloches a couple of weeks before sowing.
- Wash down the greenhouse roof and sides to remove grime.
- Clean out gutters.
- Clean and sterilize pots and trays.
- Make square mats to place around cabbage shoots from old carpet or cardboard; this will prevent cabbage root fly.
- Continue to feed the birds.
- Look for weeds beginning to emerge and start to hoe regularly – this will save you masses of time later.
- Check your overwintering herbs for any pests and diseases and remove any old stems.
- Make sure you have planned your four-year crop rotation.
- Add manure or garden compost to the potato bed.
- Use the compost from the heap to put around the beds of overwintering crops or asparagus or artichoke beds.

MARCH

The allotment is beginning to wake up. The soil begins to warm up and it is time to really get going on your allotment again. March winds and April showers bring forth May flowers.

Vegetables

Sow outdoors
Beetroot; broad beans; Brussels sprouts (sow an early variety to harvest in September, for example 'Peer Gynt' or 'Oliver'); kohlrabi; leeks; lettuce (sow outdoors from mid-March); onions; radish (sow summer varieties, such as 'French Breakfast', 'Sparkler', 'Scarlet Globe'); shallots; parsnip; perpetual spinach; early turnip (e.g. purple top Milan); peas (e.g. 'Feltham First', 'Meteor' – sow now for May/June crop).

Plant outdoors
Seakale; horseradish; onion sets; Jerusalem artichoke tubers; chitted early potatoes; shallot sets; asparagus crowns.

Sow under cover outdoors
Summer cabbage (e.g. 'Greyhound', 'Hispi', 'Primo', 'Derby Day', 'Stonehead', 'Minicole', 'Winnigstadt'); carrots (sow short-rooted varieties now for a June/July crop, e.g. 'Amsterdam Forcing', 'Early Nantes') chives; thyme; summer cauliflower; peppers; lettuce; spinach (summer varieties, e.g. 'King of Denmark', 'Medania').

Sow under heated cover
Aubergines; celery and celeriac (sow now to plant out in May/June); glasshouse cucumbers; tomatoes (sow now to plant out in May).

Start sowing under heated cover.

Start growing peppers for an early crop.

Harvest

Perpetual spinach (leaf beet); Swiss chard; early sprouting broccoli; Brussels sprouts; winter cauliflower; celeriac; chicory; endive; kale; leeks; parsnip; salsify; scorzonera; spinach; swede.

Fruit

- Finish planting bare-rooted fruit trees.
- Perpetual varieties of strawberry can be planted in March/April, e.g. 'Aromel', 'Rapella'. They can also be forced to flower by covering them with cloches. You may need to hand-pollinate them with a small paintbrush if they are covered.
- Bare-rooted canes of raspberry, blackberry, hybrid berry, blackcurrant, gooseberry can still be planted.
- Feed trees and bushes that are established.
- Train in new shoots of blackberries and loganberries on to wires.
- Protect flowers on wall-trained peaches and nectarines and pollinate them using an artist's brush if there is no sign of insect pollinators.
- Mulch with compost around the base of fruit trees, particularly young ones.
- Continue to plant grapes.
- Prune gooseberries and raspberries.

Flowers

- Sow half-hardy annuals in a heated propagator, *Lobelia* and *Tagetes* for companion planting, and anything you want to grow in summer containers and boxes.

- Pot on overwintered annuals, such as *Escholtzia*, *Calendula*, *Nigella*, etc., taking care with the tap root.
- Take cuttings of dahlias and pelargoniums.
- Plant and divide perennials.
- Divide snowdrops 'in the green'.
- Plant gladiolus corms and lily bulbs.
- Sow wildflowers under cover.

Other tasks

- Place growbags in the greenhouse to warm up.
- Clean greenhouse and cold-frame glass so that maximum light can get in.
- Begin weed-control. Hoe off annual weeds and dig out perennial ones.
- Harvest any remaining winter crops, composting the debris.
- Check trees and bushes to make sure the ties are not too tight.
- Pinch out the tops of sweet peas when they are 10cm (4in) high.
- Prepare the ground for asparagus crowns. Make sure you dig the bed deeply and incorporate plenty of organic matter, and if you have heavy clay add some horticultural grit as they need good drainage. You could consider making a raised bed for them.
- Use cloches and polythene to warm up the soil. Horticultural fleece can also be used.
- Mustard or tares can be planted on beds you are not using until May/June as a green manure (dig them in two or three weeks before using the beds).
- Cuttings can be taken from your stored dahlia tubers once they are 10cm (4in) high.

APRIL

The blossom is coming out in full force. Watch out for short, sharp frosts. The excitement begins as there is seed to sow and plants to plant.

Vegetables

Sow outdoors

Beetroot and turnip; peas and broad beans; broccoli; Brussels sprouts; cabbage; carrots; chard; endive; kale; kohlrabi; leeks; lettuce; spinach and perpetual spinach; radish; cardoons.

Sow outdoors under cover
French beans; squash (e.g. courgettes, marrows, pumpkins); greenhouse cucumbers (e.g. 'Conqueror', 'Telegraph'); lettuce; sweetcorn.

Sow under heated cover
Aubergine; celery; outdoor cucumbers (e.g. 'Burpless Tasty Green').

Plant outdoors
Globe artichoke; Jerusalem artichoke tubers; chitted potatoes (second earlies and main crops); onion and shallot sets; asparagus.

Feed fruit in containers – in this case, a fig.

Plant in greenhouse
Aubergine; peppers; tomatoes.

Fruit

- Feed fruit in containers.
- Remove the blooms from summer fruiting strawberries in their first year if planted in late autumn or early spring.
- Fruit trees are no longer dormant and so all bare-rooted fruit trees should have been planted.
- Watch out for pests on flowers and fruitlets.
- Watch out for spring frosts that can damage blossom.
- Put compost around the bottom of fruit trees.
- Keep young fruit trees well weeded; if you leave the weeds to grow they will compete for water and nutrients and the young trees cannot establish properly.
- Sow your melon seed now under cover to plant in the greenhouse in May. The best variety to plant in an unheated greenhouse is the Cantaloupe melon.
- Hand-pollination may still be required for peaches and nectarines when there are not many pollinating insects as these plants flower early.
- Don't forget to hand-pollinate strawberries if they are being forced.
- Plant and tie in new grapevines and figs.
- Check and harvest forced rhubarb.

Flowers

- It is best to wait for six weeks after the flowers of spring bulbs are over before cutting the foliage down. This allows the bulb to take in food from the leaves to prepare for next year's flowers.
- Keep planting perennial plants for flowers in the summer and finish propagating already established ones by division.
- At the end of the month it is possible to plant dormant dahlia tubers outside.
- Continue to sow hardy annuals outside.
- Plant out any hardy annuals that you sowed in autumn.
- If you have any cuttings taken from tender perennials such as pelargoniums, argaranthymums, felicias, etc, pot them up now.
- Plant spring bedding and summer bulbs.

General tasks
- Order seedlings for the vegetable and ornamental beds.
- Check and remove weeds under hedges.
- Check asparagus, artichokes and other perennial vegetables for weeds.
- If you have any plants in containers, begin regular feeding now.
- Put growbags in the greenhouse to warm up.
- Propagate perennial herbs such as rosemary, lavender, etc.
- Grass will grow very quickly in April/May, so make sure your mower is working well.

Start sowing outdoor cabbage for a good crop later.

- Before hoeing your borders, look for self-sown seedling of plants that are not weeds and could be potted up and grown on.
- Remember to harvest your forced rhubarb.
- Prepare trenches for runner beans and sweet peas; they need a good moisture-retentive soil so half-fill the trench with kitchen waste or screwed-up newspaper.

MAY

This marks the end of spring or the beginning of summer – but watch the weather. There will be lots of flowers and vegetables to harvest. Remember the best of the gardening year is still to come!

Vegetables

Sow outdoors
Runner beans; French beans (sow main crop in May with subsequent sowings to the end of June to harvest until the end of October); beetroot; broccoli; winter cabbage; Savoy cabbage; calabrese; carrots (intermediate or long-rooted varieties); cauliflower (e.g. 'Autumn Giant' – sow autumn varieties to harvest in autumn and winter varieties to harvest next spring); chicory (forcing varieties); kale; kohlrabi; lettuce; endive; courgettes, marrow, pumpkins and squash can be sown outside in late May; peas; radish; spinach (summer varieties, e.g. 'King of Denmark'); spring onions; swede; turnip (early varieties, e.g. 'Purple Top Milan').

Sow under cover
Sweetcorn.

Plant outdoors
Brussels sprouts; summer cabbage; red cabbage; celery and celeriac; leeks.

Plant out in greenhouse
Aubergine; peppers; tomatoes; cucumber (greenhouse varieties).

Harvest
Radish; asparagus; rhubarb; spinach; peas; lettuce; leeks; kale; winter cauliflower; spring cabbage; sprouting broccoli; chard.

Fruit

- Plant out alpine strawberry seedlings by the end of May.
- Feed vines with a liquid fertilizer.
- Water plants.
- Before putting straw around the strawberries to keep them clean use your form of preferred slug and snail control.
- Put codling moth traps up to prevent codling moths from mating and laying eggs in your apples.
- Protect your soft fruit from the birds by erecting a temporary fruit cage or put netting over the bushes, making sure you have access to them for picking.

Asparagus ready to harvest.

Flowers

- Take cuttings of pinks – these are called pipings and you just pull the first few sets of leaves away from the main plant and pot up. Put them in the greenhouse until they root.
- Divide primrose and polyanthus after flowering.
- Cut back plants that have flowered, such as alyssum and aubrietia. Use snips (sharp pointed scissors) to make this task easier.
- Plant out sweet peas.
- Feed spring bulbs as they finish flowering with a high potassium feed.
- Stake tall plants with pea sticks or prunings. This can be a really fun and creative job.
- You can plant out tender exotics that have been grown from cuttings at the end of the month such as cannas and dahlias.
- Protect everything from slug and snail damage.

Other tasks

- Make sure you keep seedlings watered.
- Remove any unwanted suckers from trees and shrubs as well as roses.
- Propagate perennial herbs from cuttings.
- Weeds such as bindweed, dandelions, horsetails, etc. grow very rapidly at this time of the year. Dig out their roots as soon as they appear; if not, they will set seed and spread.
- Pinch out the tops of broad beans to make them less delicious to blackfly as they love the succulent tips of these beans.
- Now is the time to cover carrot plants with fleece to prevent carrot fly.
- Tie in briar fruits regularly.
- Remove blanket weed regularly from the pond.
- Protect your young plants from slugs.
- Start to harden off plants raised in the greenhouse – bring them out in the day and in at night for a couple of weeks.

JUNE

June is just the best time to be on your allotment, with masses of vegetables and flowers to give you a lot of satisfaction. The allotment should be

By June, there should be masses of vegetables on your allotment.

teaming with wildlife and colour. Hopefully you will feel all the hard work has been worth it – take some photos just to remind you in winter how wonderful it can look.

Vegetables

Sow outdoors
French beans; beetroot; cauliflower; endive; lettuce; radish; sweetcorn; courgettes, marrows and pumpkins; runner beans; carrots; chicory; kohlrabi; peas; swede; turnips; cucumber (outdoor varieties including gherkins). Beetroot, French beans, carrots, kohlrabi, peas, lettuce, endive and radish should be sown at intervals throughout the summer months to provide you with a constant supply.

Plant outdoors
Broccoli/calabrese; runner beans; celery/celeriac; tomatoes; Brussels sprouts; summer cabbage/red cabbage; leeks. Plant out vegetables raised under cover, such as courgettes and sweetcorn.

Plant out in greenhouse
Peppers.

Plant out climbing beans.

Fruit

- Make sure fruit canes and trees are watered as the fruit is swelling.
- Cover your fruit with netting to protect them from birds.
- Thin out apples and plums. This will stop weak branches from breaking. The other thing to consider is that if you have a heavy crop one year this can result in a very small or non-existent crop the following year. This is known as biennial bearing. Thinning out your fruit will help to prevent this. Plums should be thinned to about 8-10cm (3-4in) apart, and apples a little bit further. The June drop, as it is known, is when fruit trees shed excess fruit naturally so wait until this has happened before you thin your fruit.
- Put up pheromone traps for codling moth. This will prevent moths from laying eggs in your apples. These traps are available from some garden centres and by mail order.

Flowers

- Hardy annuals can still be sown to give colour from mid-summer to autumn. Fast-growing varieties like calendula, godetia, and clarkia are a good choice; also try cosmos and zinnia, which make marvellous cut flowers and will keep going until November.
- Try to water flowers first thing in the morning or evening rather than in the hot sun, as water splashes can cause your flowers and foliage to scorch.

- Look out for the orange lily beetle. Make sure you pick them off regularly.
- Take cuttings from short-lived perennials, for example pinks and perennial wallflowers.
- If you have a greenhouse sow winter and early spring bedding plants in pots or trays.
- If you are growing flag irises (*Iris germanica*) these are best divided up in June. When they have finished flowering, divide the clump and remove the youngest pieces of rhizome, making sure they have plenty of roots, throw away the old pieces and replant them, cutting the leaves in half horizontally to avoid wind rock.

General tasks

- Water if there is no rain for long periods, but don't overwater vegetable transplants.
- Tie in sweet peas and other annual climbers regularly.
- Snap off tomato side shoots that appear in the leaf axils. These need to be checked regularly.
- Put shade netting up in the greenhouse or paint it with shading paint.
- If you are growing chrysanthemums pinch out the tips now.
- Stake gladioli.
- Mulch any bare ground with lots of organic matter. This will reduce evaporation and keep the soil moist.
- Put some compost around your asparagus plants.

Divide bearded irises.

- Hoe your plot every time you visit – even if it is only for ten minutes.
- Make sure your brassica beds are covered with very fine netting so that the cabbage white butterflies cannot fly underneath and lay their eggs.
- Insects that feed off aphids include ladybirds, lacewing larvae, hoverfly larvae, and certain predatory midges and parasitic wasps. Adults of lacewings and hoverfly feed off nectar and pollen and can be encouraged onto your plot with flowering plants. Marigolds and the poached egg plant (*Limnanthes douglasii*) are particularly effective at this. Lacewing and hoverfly attach their eggs to a plant and when the larvae hatch they eat several hundred aphids before pupating. Both the adult and larvae of the ladybird eat aphids. Ladybirds are attracted to many different plants but love eating the aphids that appear on nettles.
- Watch out for pigeons and take the appropriate precautions, e.g. netting or any other methods that will scare them away!

JULY

July is that time when you just want to be outside all the time. When it is sunny all the flowers open and the evening fills the air with perfume. Try to

Limnanthes douglasii *(poached egg plant) makes a good landing pad for hoverflies.*

Sow some parsley for winter use.

spend some evenings at your allotment to enjoy the honeysuckle, nicotiana and other night-scented plants, and to watch the moths doing their work.

Vegetables

Sow outdoors
Spring cabbage (to harvest next spring); non-forcing varieties of chicory (e.g. 'Sugar Loaf'); Chinese cabbage; endive; kohlrabi; lettuce; parsley; peas; radish; turnip; French beans; beetroot; carrot. Sow some parsley for winter use.

Plant outdoors
Broccoli/calabrese; cauliflower; kale; leeks; cabbage (winter and savoy). Autumn and winter salad vegetables can be sown now; winter purslane, corn salad or lamb's lettuce and rocket are happy in most situations. Except for land cress, all these can be treated as cut-and-come-again. You can get as many as four cuttings from each crop. When they reach a few centimetres high cut them with snips then wait for the next few centimetres to grow and then cut them again.

Harvest
Globe artichokes; broad beans; French beans; some early runner beans; Swiss chard; perpetual spinach; summer cabbage; carrot; cauliflower (summer varieties); beetroot; greenhouse cucumbers; kohlrabi; lettuce; courgette and other summer squash; onions; shallots; garlic; peas; potatoes (first earlies); radish; spinach; the first greenhouse tomatoes.

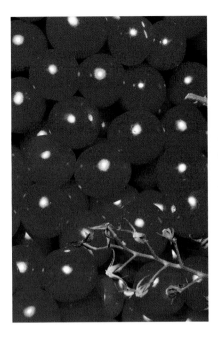

Harvest the first greenhouse tomatoes in July.

Fruit

- A lot of cane fruit will be ripening in July so make sure you keep the fruit well watered while the fruits are swelling.
- Apple trees can be pruned in July – this reduces the vegetative growth of the tree by restricting the food supply through photosynthesis.
- Summer-fruiting raspberries should be pruned after harvesting. Cut all the old fruited canes down to the ground. Tie this year's new canes into the wire supports.
- Summer pruning of redcurrants, whitecurrants and gooseberries should be done in July. The side shoots, which are this year's growth, should be pruned to three or four buds. Cut out any shoots that are crossing or growing into the middle of the bush.
- Strawberries should have all their old leaves cut off after harvesting has finished. Use a pair of shears for this job. You can compost any old leaves and straw, but don't forget to remove any weeds at the same time.

Harvest
Blackcurrants; gooseberries; rhubarb; some strawberry varieties; summer-fruiting raspberries; redcurrants; cherries; peaches.

Flowers

- Deadhead perennials; follow the dead flower stem right back down into the crown of the plant, and cut if off just above the basal cluster of leaves. If there is a side shoot part of the way down the main stem that still has flower buds on it to come, make sure you cut just above the junction with it.
- Plant autumn flowering bulbs such as nerine, cyclamens and autumn crocus.
- You can cut hardy geraniums and oriental poppies down to the ground and then they will flower again in a few weeks time.
- If you are growing violas cut back the straggly growth to encourage new shoots and then you can take cuttings to increase your stock for next year.

General tasks
- Make sure you deadhead all your plants frequently. A plant flowers and sets seed for survival and annuals will soon die if they are just left, so take some snips and deadhead all your plants regularly. This will prolong their life by months.
- Put out some water for birds and hedgehogs if there has been no rain.
- Pinch out the side shoots of tomatoes, and growing tips after the fourth tress has set. (That means the fourth 'bunch' of tomatoes). This forces the plants to put their energy into the ripening process.
- Harvest herbs for drying and storing.
- Use a high potassium feed on tomato plants weekly and keep them well watered. Dryness around the roots prevents the tomato plants from taking up sufficient calcium and can cause blossom end rot.
- Keep your onions well weeded. Onions, due to their upright habit, do not suppress weeds well, unlike potatoes that produce a lot of foliage. This is why it is a good idea for crop rotation purposes to grow onions on ground previously occupied by potatoes. Give your onions a feed at the same time.
- Check your brassicas for any signs of caterpillars of the cabbage white butterfly. Look

under the leaves as well for the egg.

- Watch out for carrot fly.
- Pinch out runner beans once they reach the top of their support.
- Protect potatoes from the blight by cover the soil with a thick mulch.
- Ensure there is good ventilation in the greenhouse and leave the doors and windows open for as long as possible each day.
- Try to pull out weeds before they go to seed.
- Make arrangements for someone to look after your allotment when you go away on holiday. Reward them with free fruit and vegetables on your return. Don't forget to tell them that the runner beans need lots of water to encourage the flowers to set at this time of year.

AUGUST

August is the time to sit back and enjoy your allotment. Plants are very forgiving and things will come up again next year; and if not, you can plant some more. So really enjoy August and have a feast with all the fruit, vegetables and flowers you have produced.

Vegetables

Sow outdoors
Lettuce (sow hardy varieties, e.g. 'Winter Density', for next spring); Japanese onions (sow seed to harvest early next summer – sets are planted later); parsley (protect from carrot root fly); spring cabbage; Chinese cabbage; endive; kohlrabi; winter radish; spinach; turnip.

Plant outdoors
Savoy cabbage; kale.

Fruit

- Keep making sure that fruit trees, bushes and cane fruit are kept well watered.
- You can prune mature plum trees after fruiting. If there is any sign of silver leaf, cut several centimetres past any brown-stained wood and make sure you burn the prunings. If any branches are broken or overcrowded cut these out.
- Summer prune cordon apples and pears. The

side shoot growing from the main stem should be cut back to 7.5cm (3in). Those shoots pruned this way last year will have produced smaller side shoots, which should be cut back to 2.5cm (1in). This encourages the formation of short fruit-bearing spurs for next year.

- Cut out old canes from raspberry plants after fruiting.
- Summer prune gooseberries and redcurrants.
- Plant new strawberry plants and remove those that are more than three years old. You can use the runners to propagate new plants. Put the runner, still attached to the parent plant, into flowerpots and bury them half way up in the ground; when they have rooted remove them from the parent plant.
- If you are growing melons support the fruits with nets or old tights.
- Check that trees laden with fruit are supported to stop the branches from snapping off.

Harvest
Apples; pears; strawberries; blackberries; raspberries; gooseberries; peaches; apricots; cherries; melons; plums; redcurrants.

Flowers

- Buddleia is a fantastic plant to grow on your allotment as at this time of year it attracts many butterflies, including comma, peacock, red

Melons need to be supported with nets.

Ripe plums ready for harvesting.

admiral and small tortoiseshell as it produces lots of nectar that smells delicious.

- Annuals that have finished flowering can be pulled out and put on the compost heap.
- Propagate tender perennials including fuchsias and pelargoniums by taking cuttings of healthy non-flowering shoots.
- Plant daffodils and narcissi at the end of the month.
- Cut and dry everlasting flowers.
- Save the seeds of hardy annuals before composting the plants.

General tasks
- Finish trimming evergreen hedges.
- Lift, dry and store garlic.
- Thin out overcrowded water lily leaves in the pond.
- Top up the pond in dry spells.
- Keep on top of weeds to make sure they do not go to seed.
- Bindweed is at its peak now. Try to trace it back to its source and remove it.
- Earth up potatoes to prevent any blight spores reaching the tubers.
- If carrots show signs of attack from carrot fly, remove them.
- Make a rack on which to dry your onions and garlic using chicken wire attached to a frame.
- As soon as the ground becomes vacant, plant green manures. Rape and mustard sown in August can be dug into the soil in the autumn.

However, they are brassicas and you must remember they are susceptible to the same diseases as other family members.
- Give broccoli plenty of water when their heads are forming.
- Cut and dry herbs for winter use.
- Earth up or wrap blanching varieties of celery and make sure they get plenty of water.
- Deadhead annuals.
- Watch out for vine weevils and squash any you see; inspect pots for the grubs.

SEPTEMBER

September is a really rewarding month, with the harvest to gather and so many berries and fruits to enjoy. The light is remarkable at this time of the year with shafts of low light and lots of flowers such as dahlias, gingers, cannas and other hot-coloured plants as well as grasses looking splendid.

Vegetables

Sow outside
Lettuce (sow hardy varieties, e.g. 'Winter Density' or 'Valor'); parsley; spinach.
Plant outside
Spring cabbage; onion sets (plant 'Japanese' or overwintering varieties for June); garlic.

Flowers in September light.

An apple tree laden with fruit.

Harvest

Globe artichokes; aubergine; broad beans;
French beans; runner beans; Swiss chard;
beetroot; calabrese; broccoli; summer cabbage;
red cabbage; peppers; carrots; cauliflower; celery;
cucumber; endive; kohlrabi; lettuce; courgettes;
squash; pumpkins; onions; shallots; peas;
mangetout; potatoes (main crop); radish; spinach;
sweetcorn; tomatoes; turnips.

Fruit

- Prune your mature plum trees after fruiting.
  Remove any branches infected by silver leaf
  fungus. Burn the prunings.
- Apple and pear trees can still be summer
  pruned.
- Apples and pears should be harvested when the
  fruit separates easily from the branch.
- Check fruit and if there is any sign of rot throw
  them away.
- Keep windfalls in a box to put out for birds in
  winter as blackbirds, thrushes, redwings and
  fieldfares will enjoy a feast of fruit when it is
  cold.
- Fix grease bands round apple trees to trap the
  female winter moths.
- Plant strawberries by the end of the month.

Harvest

Apples; pears; plums; peaches; nectarines; figs;
strawberries; blackberries; raspberries; early
melons; grapes.

Flowers

- Continue to pick dahlias and they will reward
  you with many more flowers for a few weeks
  yet.
- Plant spring bulbs, but wait until next month or
  even November to plant tulips and hyacinths.
- Collect seeds from perennials and alpines. Put
  them in a paper bag; it is best to leave the seeds
  to ripen on the plant and then collect them.
  Store in a cool dry place and sort them out on a
  cold winter night by the fire.
- Replace the summer bedding when it is finished
  with winter and spring bedding such as pansies
  and polyanthus.

General tasks

- Keep up the watering and deadheading.
- Lift maincrop potatoes – remove haulms
  (the above ground green parts) several weeks
  before lifting if they have blight.
- Cut down the stems of perennial plants that
  have flowered to keep the borders tidy as the
  later flowers take over.
- Cut down the asparagus foliage and mulch the
  ground well.
- Keep weeding.
- Continue to feed tomatoes weekly.
- Keep checking for caterpillars on brassicas.
- Get your compost heap going as there will be a

*Continue to pick
dahlias into
September.*

Saving seeds for next year.

lot of waste to add this month. Try to layer it so you get a good carbon/nitrogen balance.

- Plant green manure as the beds become vacant.
- It will help tomato plants to ripen if you lay them down over some straw and cover them with cloches. You can also hang banana skins above your tomatoes in the greenhouse to aid ripening.
- Stake mature Brussels sprout plants.
- Lift, divide and replant early spring flowering perennials.

OCTOBER

The leaves are glowing red, yellow, orange and crimson and are beginning to fall. Watch out for frost if you live in the north-east. October is the beginning of a new season with a multitude of colours and textures. Keep gardening. Harvest berries and use them to make jams and preserves.

Vegetables

Sow outside
Broad beans for an early spring crop; winter hardy lettuce (e.g. 'Winter Density'); oriental greens, such as mizuna, pak choi, green-in-snow, giant red mustard, mibuna. These are all very hardy and will grow outside or in the greenhouse.

Plant outside
Spring cabbage; garlic; onion sets (overwintering or 'Japanese' varieties); kale.

Harvest
Jerusalem artichokes; aubergine; sweet potatoes; French beans; runner beans; Swiss chard; beetroot; calabrese; broccoli; Brussels sprouts; summer cabbage; red cabbage; Savoy cabbage; peppers; carrots; cauliflower; celeriac; celery; chicory (non-forcing varieties); cucumber; endive; kohlrabi; leeks (early varieties); lettuce; squash; courgettes; pumpkins; peas; potatoes (main crop); radish; salsify; scorzonera; spinach; swede; tomatoes; turnips.

Fruit

- Plant rhubarb crowns.
- Prune summer-fruiting raspberries. Cut down the canes that have just fruited and tie the best unfruited canes to supports.
- Order new fruit trees.
- Cut out the old canes of tayberries, loganberries and blackberries and ties in the new ones.
- Propagate blackcurrants, red- and whitecurrants and gooseberries. Take a 30cm (12in) shoot just above a bud on the parent plant. Remove the top 5cm (2in). Plant the cutting into a bed through some black polythene, burying two thirds of the cutting.

Harvest
Apples; pears; autumn-fruiting raspberries; melons; grapes.

Squash harvest.

Flowers

- Plant out spring bedding plants such as forget-me-nots and wallflowers by the end of the month.
- Any annuals such as busy Lizzies can be potted up and put in the greenhouse to keep going; they are great for children to take cuttings from and keep as house plants. Just cut a stem and put it in a jar of water and watch it develop roots.
- Chocolate cosmos, gladioli, cannas, etc., should either be lifted and stored in a frost-free place or a thick mulch put over them to keep them snug over winter. This will depend on where you live. If you have a lot and you give them a really good mulch they should survive the winter underground.
- Perennials that flowered earlier can be lifted and divided – give some to your allotment neighbour, and it will stand you in good stead for those watering favours you will need next year! Late-flowering perennials are best left to divide in spring.

General tasks

- Lift maincrop potatoes two weeks after the tops have died or been cut down. Make sure the potatoes are dry before storing them in paper sacks.
- Earth up celery to blanch the stems, making them more tender.

Bring in tender plants and tidy up the greenhouse for next year.

Place water butts to collect rain water from shed roofs.

- Collect leaves. Make a container from four posts with chicken wire around the sides attached to the posts. It will take about eighteen months for the leaves to be ready to add to the soil. They make a great soil supplement.
- Lift, divide and replant old clumps of rhubarb. You could grow some in your flower bed, as it is a beautiful plant.
- Move frost-tender plants into the greenhouse.
- Generally tidy up the borders.
- Reduce ventilation in the greenhouse.
- Place water butts to collect rainwater from the roofs of sheds and any other buildings.
- Cover your compost bins to keep the rain out and the heat in.
- Clear out the pond. Cut down any dying leaves from marginal plants.
- If your allotment is on a clay soil or in a wet area begin the winter digging.
- Remove yellowing leaves from winter brassicas as they encourage mould.

NOVEMBER

This is the time to think about preparing for the wintertime. Don't neglect your allotment now; keep going regularly and be inspired by the colours and scents of autumn days. If you work your allotment now it will provide a really good foundation for next year.

Vegetables

Sow outside

Broad beans; peas such as 'Feltham First' and 'Meteor'.

Plant outside

Garlic cloves such as 'Thermidrome' and 'Printantor' seem to grow well in the United Kingdom.

Harvest

Jerusalem artichokes; perpetual spinach; Brussels sprouts; winter cabbage; Savoy cabbage; red cabbage; carrots; cauliflower; celeriac; celery; chicory (no-forcing and forcing varieties); endive; kale; leeks; lettuce; parsnip; pumpkins; radish; salsify; scorzonera; spinach; swede; turnips.

Fruit

- Plant rhubarb crowns.
- Cut the fruited canes of autumn-fruiting raspberries right down to the ground. It is best to burn the prunings to prevent any diseases spreading.
- Prepare the ground for planting new bush fruits. After digging and incorporating plenty of organic matter, use a weed-suppressing fabric to put over the ground. You can then plant your fruit bushes through the fabric. This will keep the weeds down. Add some bark chippings to keep the fabric from blowing away; it may also need pinning down with wire.

Harvest

Apples; pears; autumn-fruiting raspberries.

Flowers

- Pick seed heads to display in the house, together with autumn berries.
- Harvest gourds and varnish them for Christmas.
- Mulch any tender plants, such as agapanthus, to overwinter.
- Continue to plant tulips and hyacinths.
- Dig up your dahlia tubers and store in a dry place.
- Plant lily bulbs.
- Take dead leaves from the tops of plants as they may spread disease.

General tasks

- If you are on a clay soil it is good to dig in manure in the autumn and then it can be broken down and incorporated over the winter.
- If your allotment is on a sandy or chalky soil, wait until the spring as the nutrients added by the manure will be washed out over the winter.
- Green manure can be dug into the soil.
- If you have a wormery, insulate it with bubble wrap.
- Check any crops you have in store to detect any rot.
- Net your Brussels sprouts and broccoli to protect them from pigeons.
- Check your allotment for anything that will suffer from the elements. For example cold, wind or waterlogging, and take the appropriate action.

Further information

USEFUL CONTACTS

Federation of City Farms and Community
Gardens (provides advice for allotment societies)
0117 923 1800
www.farmgarden.org.uk

National Society of Allotment and Leisure
Gardeners (NSALG)
01536 266 576
www.nsalg.org.uk

The Soil Association (supports local groups)
0117 914 2425
www.soilassociation.org.uk/localgroups

SEED SUPPLIERS

Edwin Tucker and Sons (large packs and old
favourites)
01364 652 233
www.tucker-seeds.co.uk

Franchi Seeds of Italy (traditional and regional
Italian varieties)
020 8427 5020
www.seedsofitaly.com

Kings Seeds (wide choice of vegetables and
flower seeds, including sweet peas)
01376 570 00
www.kingsseeds.com

Marshalls (great for potatoes)
01480 443 390
www.marshalls-seeds.co.uk

The Organic Gardening Catalogue (heritage and
modern seeds)
0845 130 1304
www.organiccatalogue.com

Index